The Modern Couple

by
Andrew
and
Helen Jackson

urbanpress

The Modern Couple
by Andrew and Helen Jackson
Copyright ©2017 Andrew and Helen Jackson

ISBN 978-1-63360-055-3
For Worldwide Distribution
Printed in the U.S.A.

Urban Press
P.O. Box 8882
Pittsburgh, PA 15221-0882
412.646.2780

TABLE OF CONTENTS

INTRODUCTION

It is easy to criticize the Federal Government, and people from both political parties do just that, complaining that the government does too much, too little, or the wrong things. In 2004, however, the U.S. Government did one good thing that changed the course of our lives and ministry. A local organization received a government grant to establish a program to strengthen modern couples, and we found ourselves in a class to be trained as workshop facilitators for a program in Pittsburgh called The Marriage Works (TMW).

After our training, we went out to local churches to conduct ten-week training courses for couples, whether they were married or not. Since it was a government-funded program, our workshop material was not overtly spiritual, but being in a church setting led to lots of questions, and then we were permitted to discuss our faith. It was a wonderful season when we both were able to focus on what we believed was and is part of our calling, and that is to counsel and equip modern couples for marital success.

As happens with many government grants, the funding disappears as newly-elected officials institute programs in line with their priorities, so eventually The Marriage Works ended and everything went into hibernation. Then we became pastors in the urban community, specifically in the Hill District of Pittsburgh, and we were immediately confronted with the need for TMW program. Thanks to a grant from our sister church in Pittsburgh, Allegheny Center Alliance Church, we were able to find the workshop material that was stored away, supplement it with our own faith-based material, and begin anew to offer workshops for couples. It was rewarding to be doing workshops again, but this time with biblical material as a central part of our presentation.

Now we have seen the need to write this book to make the material even more accessible to couples not just in Pittsburgh, but all around the world. Our goal to write this book to help modern couples in their relationships and equip them with principles and lessons that will keep their relationships together and strengthen the entire family unit.

The name The Marriage Works is in use by another organization, so we have renamed our material *The Modern Couple,* and have assembled this book as a tool for couples to reference real-life examples of what a positive and healthy marriage looks like. Notice we did not say perfect marriage, for there is no such thing as a perfect marriage. We want to answer the question: What does a *healthy* marriage look like? In the process, we will cover things like conflict resolution, effective communication, decision making, and budgeting—just to name a few. We will provide copious personal examples and illustrations so you will see a modern couple in an urban setting working out their difficulties without resorting to divorce as a way out. Along the way, we hope to be funny and witty, but also provide a helpful resource to which you can refer. And, oh yes, we will be talking about sex.

We have been married for more than 26 years and have been friends longer than that. We believe we have a unique perspective of not only how to enhance a marriage or relationship, but also how to stay friends as we have through the years. We must say at the start that we believe God instituted marriage. As pastors and ministers, we believe we have a responsibility to help others build model relationships for the community and for their families and friends to see and emulate.

As pastors, we feel God has called us to do this. We know that to be true because of the success we have had in helping others. In fact, we have seen God send us couples who didn't know why they were coming to us, but when they came, it was clear they needed marital help. Part of our calling has been to demonstrate what a healthy Christian marriage looks like. During our time as pastors, we've seen too many divorces and bad relationships, so we feel compelled to do what we can to correct the problem on whatever level we can.

We also believe we are called to be agents of change. This book you are holding is meant to create a change in how people feel about marriage. In the community where we pastor, we have a high percentage of couples who live together, and that's unacceptable. For many of those modern couples, marriage isn't even a consideration for a number of reasons. We need to help effect a positive change where people are actually looking forward to getting and staying married.

When we were growing up, girls began to think about getting married at a young age. They asked themselves and even dreamt about what they were going to look like as a bride, what they were going to wear. What happened to that kind of thinking? We don't simply want to provide a manual for marriage, but to actually change the thinking in our culture that marriage is a positive thing.

Let's get even more specific. Our church is located in a high-crime, low-income area of Pittsburgh in which 71% of the people in that area are unmarried. That's almost a number that's hard to believe, but it's a fact. What we offer is desperately needed. The other statistic that jumps out at us is that almost all of the children of single parents are living in a household whose income is below the poverty level. The same study showed that when a husband and wife stay together, the percentage of families living at or below the poverty level goes down by 82%.

In other words, when couples are together, people are *not* living at the poverty level. We know when people are under that poverty level, it brings a lot of other issues into play. We did a lot of other research and found that these same children who live below the poverty level have a higher school dropout rate, more teen pregnancies, and a lot of other problems that are directly related to the family unit, or absence of it. It's our belief that if we can see the family unit healed and restored, a lot of other problems will take care of themselves.

While we are marriage advocates, we love working with couples on whatever level they are—whether they are dating, married, getting ready to be married, or cohabiting. We want to show them—and show you in this book—how to have a better relationship by doing things God's way. Even if you are cohabiting, some of the tools in this book will eventually lead you to get married and then to live in a way that is pleasing in God's sight. We're not making the book exclusively for the married, though it's one of our primary objectives. We want any modern couple to read this book and have their relationship enhanced.

We have already alluded to how this book can be used, but let's be more specific. First, we would like to see churches and other organizations use it as a training tool to conduct their own workshop sessions. We don't want it to be too clinical because we are not acting as marriage counselors, but rather as marriage enrichment facilitators and relationship enhancers. We want to help those who are not only in trouble, but those who have good marriages to make them even better. And as we stated, we hope you will refer back to this book again and again to pick up tips that will refresh and stimulate you to improve your life together.

We had a couple who had been married for more than 50 years who went through the TMW program. They came into the course to help us out, or so they thought. They had been married for so long and been through so many things that they thought they pretty much had a handle on everything. They learned through the program, however, new ways of interacting with each other and how they could do some things even better than before. Because they were members in our church, they came to one of our church's movie nights holding hands. The course seemed to spark something in them and was part of that enrichment objective we have in mind to accomplish for married couples.

Now let's begin this book with both of us telling you our stories and giving you our backgrounds so you know who we are. It goes without saying that we are not writing because we have the ideal marriage. We would like to think it is a good marriage, and we have a lot of pastoral experience in sharing important marriage principles with others. Let's now get started on this journey to help you, the modern couple, have a vibrant, loving relationship in the tumultuous times of the 21st century.

Andrew and Helen Jackson
Pittsburgh, PA
January 2017

CHAPTER 1

JACK'S STORY

I was born and raised in Pittsburgh in an area called South Oakland. I grew up in the shadow of the Cathedral of Learning and Forbes Field, where the Pittsburgh Pirates baseball team used to play. Growing up in South Oakland, my main focus in life was playing ball. I was always in search of a basketball court, football field, or baseball diamond. We lived very close to a ball field, so my mother never had any trouble finding me because I was always there playing ball. By the way, my first name is Andrew, but many people still call me by my nickname of Jack.

My parents are transplanted Southerners from Arkansas. My dad and mom came to Pittsburgh in the late '40s, right after the War. Dad served in the War, and then they moved to Pittsburgh to find work opportunities. Dad landed a job in the J&L Steel Mill, where he worked until he retired, something like 40-odd years. My mother did domestic work. There were advantages to being a domestic, for the kids anyways. When the people she worked for would clean out their closets, we got their clothes and that's how we dressed. Mom served in that capacity off and on for many years.

Both my parents were staunch Baptists. As kids, we were in church every time the church door opened. My dad did a lot of work for the church and he served as a big influence on my life. He devoted himself to the church and was quite generous with his money and time. We didn't have a lot, but it seemed like we never ran out of anything, in spite of how much Dad gave away. I remember one time when a man came by the house and he was hungry. My dad always kept meat in the freezer, but he didn't give him the meat. Dad gave him the whole freezer! My brothers and I looked at each other wondering if he was kidding and what we were supposed to eat after that. That was our thought, but we never wanted for anything. That's the kind of guy my dad was.

I graduated from Schenley High School, where I wasn't the best of students. I had some issues while I was in school, but I did manage to graduate and went through a lot of changes in the next 20-plus years. I married at an early age (when I was 19 years old), and my wife at the time was 17. I had just graduated from high school and we were young with few life skills or any foundation that helped us understand how to relate to one another, so we ended up getting a divorce after 12 years. From that union came three children. I was single for 10 years after that before I married my current and *last* wife, Helen. We've been married now for 26 years. I had an early-in-life call to leadership in the church. After I graduated from high school, however, I didn't want to be a part of the church scene any longer. Even though I grew up in a church-going family, I decided I was never going back to church again. As it worked out, it was 20 years before I went back to church.

A big reason why I finally went back was because I was dating my wife, Helen, and one of her stipulations was that if I wanted to date her, I had to go to church. I figured, "What's a couple of hours on Sunday in return for spending time with her?" I knew I could still do what I wanted after church. We had a traditional old school courtship where sex wasn't involved before marriage, and that was a shock to my way of thinking at that time. During our courtship, however, I learned a lot about myself. Most important was that I realized I wanted to be married. We eventually got married and here we are today—parents, grandparents, teachers, students, pastors, and marriage growth facilitators.

I have had various jobs during my adult years. Presently, I am a bi-vocational pastor, working a full-time job as the facilities director at Reformed Presbyterian Theological Seminary in Pittsburgh. I took that job after I retired from a facilities management position at the University of Pittsburgh. I was off for a year and the president of the seminary made me an offer I couldn't refuse, so I came back to work. I've been a truck driver, a landscaper, and a lot of other things. You name the job and I've probably worked it over the years. I was a truck driver for the larger part of my adult life.

I mentioned that I sensed a call to ministry early in life. As I look back, the call was on my life as early as the 12th grade. When I heard it, however, I ran from it, up until I was 36 years old. One day, I was probably at the lowest point in my life and found myself with nowhere to go and nothing to do but to look to the Lord for help. At that point, I didn't know if that was my call to preach, but I felt the call to at least reestablish my relationship with the Lord. I knew I wanted to work in the church, so I went to my pastor at the time and asked if I could just usher. That was enough for me at the time, but I found myself getting more and more deeply involved in church. The next thing I knew, I was a deacon, then eventually I was the chairman of the deacons. That's when I sensed a clear, powerful call to pastoral ministry. The call was not so much to preach, but towards evangelism and outreach ministry. That's how I really got started in ministry work.

I passed over my divorce pretty quickly, but let me say that it was a painful time for me, although at the time, I wouldn't admit it. The more I look back on it, however, I realize the most pain came from my feeling like I was a failure. My children were still pretty young, and I was separated from them at a time when they needed me. Our circumstances didn't allow me to be as involved in their lives as I wanted or needed to be.

Currently, I am the pastor at the Webster Avenue Christian and Missionary Alliance Church, located in the Hill District of Pittsburgh. The church is in an area that really needs to be evangelized. We are surrounded by three large Baptist churches, but I think we have a valuable role to play in the community. I've been there for five years as of this writing, and we are starting to see growth.

Before I acknowledged and accepted my call, I was drinking heavily. I can remember one time waking up and not remembering anything that had gone on or what I had done. As funny as it may sound, I heard the Lord speak directly to my heart. His voice wasn't audible, but it was a sound I recognized had been in my life all along. He whispered to me that He loved me and that I could do better. By this time, I had bottomed out. It wasn't the first time I heard the voice say I could be doing better, but it was the time that convinced me I had to change my ways.

When the Lord called me, it wasn't like the Fourth of July with a lot of fireworks. It was quiet and provided direction, "This is what I want you to do." I talked it over with my wife and my father, who has since passed, and I acknowledged that I had a burning desire to minister. Out of that, something called Abundant Mercy Ministries was born, started as an evangelistic outreach ministry. I believe that's still one of my primary calls—evangelism.

I didn't have any education outside of high school, and it weighed heavily on me as I went into the ministry. Therefore, after 35 years of being away from school, I went back to earn a degree at Geneva College at the Center for Urban Biblical Ministry, where I eventually earned my associate degree in Christian Ministry. As I write, I am close to finishing my bachelor's degree in Christian Ministry.

This book represents another aspect of my call to ministry, for it emanates from my own painful mistakes where my marriage relationship is concerned. I want to equip modern couples with the wisdom and knowledge I have gained, and help my community cure some of its long-standing problems that stem from fatherlessness and broken relationships. Now I will let my wife tell you her story before we move into the lessons that make up most of this book.

CHAPTER 2

HELEN'S STORY

I grew up in Pittsburgh, and refer to myself as a Pittsburgh girl, since I've lived here all my life. Unlike my husband who has deep roots in one community, I grew up moving all around the city of Pittsburgh—north, south, east, and west. I spent my young years in the Homewood section, which in those days was called Homewood-Brushton. I went through grade school in that area and then we relocated. If you know anything about Pittsburgh, you know that the city is famous for new development coming into a community and uprooting the residents, with the hopes the residents will come back when it's all developed. Normally that does not happen, which was the case when I was growing up.

We were transplanted to the South Side of Pittsburgh, which was predominately an ethnic, Caucasian community. It was a steel mill neighborhood and all that came with that designation. We lived in the housing projects, went to high school in that community, and learned so much through that experience that I wouldn't trade for anything in the world. I loved growing up there.

I opened my first bank account at the South Side Mellon Bank when I was 16 years old. I got my first job there when I was 14 years old, earning the huge sum of 80 cents an hour. I played sports with the first African American, all-girls Catholic basketball team at St. John's, which was a great experience. All in all, I had a healthy, wonderful childhood. I grew up in a Christian home, but not a perfect home.

I was taught the Christian way and schooled in Bible lessons to help me know the Lord, whom I invited into my life at an early age. My mother had some demons, however, and she dealt with alcoholism, which in those days most people didn't discuss openly or for which she did not seek help, especially since she was raising me as a single mother. I didn't ever mention her problem or tell people that my mother drank herself into stupors, so I learned to look good while I felt bad.

I lived through that with her, but I am glad to report that she came through it when the Lord delivered her. After that, I watched her live out her years until she passed away healthy, clean, and delivered, while serving the Lord. I went on from that experience and moved to South Oakland, which is where I met my husband. I remember the first time I saw him and can still picture exactly what he had on. I looked at him and knew we were going to have some sort of connection. That is important because I had expectations of being married and in a healthy marriage, so that's pretty much what I was looking forward to having.

I graduated from South High School and went to Point Park College, which wasn't a university then. I majored in journalism and communications, thinking I was going to be on television and have my own talk show—and that was before Oprah was around. I saw myself rich and thought that was the kind of the lifestyle I was going to have. I was traveling down that road but made a detour when I had a baby while I was in college. Back then, the month of January was when we took spring break, so I spent one break in New York City at Rockefeller Center. I came back to Pittsburgh and had my baby. I was devastated because I felt I had let everyone in my family down, since no one in my family had gone to college. I had wanted to go so badly because I had such a dominant picture inside me of exactly what I wanted to do and be. My pregnancy occurred, however, and I wasn't going to finish college.

From that point on, I began to drink. I was depressed, and I didn't know what else to do. No one in our culture went and got a prescription for something like Xanax or Ambien to relieve depression. We simply went and got a bottle of whiskey or wine. I didn't know there were drugs to treat that, so I traveled down that road. I remember looking out of my third-floor window in the housing projects and seeing the Cathedral of Learning, the University of Pittsburgh's tall classroom and administration building. I asked God to help me just a little to be able to attend the University. I promised to work five jobs and do whatever I had to do if He would just get me out of where I was so I would never have to come back. I didn't want to get married and raise children in that environment.

Little did I know that later I would move into a home my father owned on Frazier Street that was not far from that Cathedral. It was a huge 13-room house, which was overwhelming, but I loved it. I worked a job with the county government for 32 years and I thought I would do that until I raised my son and retired. I was doing well, but my life wasn't completely fulfilled because I was looking to be married. I made peace with that, telling myself that if it didn't happen, it would be okay because I had a wonderful job. I found out about Geneva College at the Center for Urban Biblical Ministry and knew I wanted to go back and complete my degree because that was my heart's desire.

I was finally able to attend and had a professor who wouldn't let me move on without knowing what my purpose is. Every five minutes, or so it seemed, he would talk to me about purpose. He would tell me, "I can't believe you are in that job. How long have you been in that job? You're in the wrong place." This man kept talking about purpose and it was getting on my nerves. I couldn't really see myself doing anything else than what I was doing. One day, however, the job just wasn't working for me any longer. I decided I should take a long look at my life, and decided to continue my educational experience. I went through to a master's degree and then came back to the Center for Urban Biblical Ministry to teach and recruit.

As Jack told you, we have been married for more than 26 years. I was married once before, but during that time I was depressed and without any direction. I never lost sight of my goals, but I had concluded that I couldn't reach them. So I made some poor decisions that caused me to believe I deserved to be where I was at. Consequently, I stopped reaching and settled for where I was, which was "good enough." That caused me to enter into a marriage that was quite a mismatch, and wasn't a healthy place for me. This gentleman was a nice man, but we didn't hold the same Christian values and he wasn't a sold-out believer. That marriage lasted only four years.

Then I met the most wonderful person who was like a savior to me. Andrew Jackson had a lot of strength, wisdom, fortitude, and stamina. He was strong and still is a safe place for me. He never had a problem telling me something important. I never had a problem with him telling me what he thought or the right way to do something. We first came together after Jack had lost his middle brother, Barney, who was the same age as I. I knew Barney growing up and we saw one another at the bus stop all the time. We both were working retail back then, so all of the retail people gathered at the back of the bus to talk about their day. We rode the bus for years together and became good friends and lived four doors down from each other.

When Barney passed away in his early thirties, Jack wasn't my husband at that point, but I could see the pain and hurt in him and how he was saddened by Barney's passing. One thing I did not mention was that I had a brother thirteen years older than I who passed away when I was 20. Just when I got to the adult age where I could relate well to him and be friends, he passed away. I was his little princess, so I could really identify with what Jack was going through in terms of losing a brother. In those community neighborhoods, everyone came to the church for the wake, so I came to offer my condolences. I went to pay my respects and we began to interact from then on. I really wanted to share the love of the Lord with Jack. That was something I knew, so I wanted to say I knew how he felt that day when I saw him, and assure him that the love of the Lord would come into his heart and life if he let Him. We've been together ever since that moment and have never separated.

As in all marriages, we've had our ups and downs. As a matter of fact, shortly after anyone says "I do" is when the challenges are going to start. That's another reason why I think we're qualified to write this book, because we have dealt with life together where we have seen the good and the bad, had our financial and health ups and downs. The one good thing is that we're best friends, so even when we couldn't get along as husband and wife, our friendship held us together. That's some of what we want to express in this book. We've gone through some ups and downs, but now the down doesn't seem as bad as it used to be, because we're working on those down times together. We have a blended family with five kids altogether and 12 grandkids. If I regret anything in our 26 years of marriage, it's that it's not closer to 40 years of marriage, because we could have avoided a lot of grief and anguish if we would have met earlier.

Jack had a vision of owning and having his own cleaning business. When I heard that, I thought, "You've got to be kidding me? I don't want to be cleaning anything." He had a vison for a commercial cleaning company, and Jack had every detail mapped out. It first started with power washing, which I didn't understand at all. Then the Lord took it another way and gave him the name "All-Pro Cleaning Services." I came up with a tagline, "It's a dirty world, but someone has to clean it," which we put on our business cards. From there, the Lord opened all kinds of doors for us. People called us and we never had to work or market to get contracts. At our peak, we had more than 40 clients with 13 employees. Jack also started a summer youth program at our church where the youth could come and work for us and earn money to buy school clothes and supplies. We did well and made a lot of money. I enjoyed hiring the youth and having them work for us. It was great and God was in it, and then God moved us on to something else.

Before I met Jack, I vowed I was never going to get married again. Finding and marrying Jack, however, was just what I needed. Adjusting to married life again wasn't difficult for me. That's in part because of the prior marriage experience we had. We had learned what *not* to do and had learned from our mistakes. Plus, we had an effective courtship. We didn't just jump in the sack. We took it slow and got to know one another. After a brief period of time, it was like we had been together forever. Just as God had preordained marriage for Adam with Eve and Isaac with Rebekah, I believe our marriage was ordained by God as well.

One of the more difficult transitions for me when we got married was including someone else in my decision-making process. I had been a single parent and was raised in a single-parent home. I was accustomed to not having a father or husband around. My mother was a strong woman with a strong will. She could switch hats and be the disciplinarian or the nurturer in the blink of an eye. That's what I was used to, and that's how I was. I wasn't really used to yielding and submitting. I wasn't against doing that, I just didn't have much experience doing it.

When we got married, my son was 12 and one of Jack's sons was 13. Those two had grown up as buddies before we married. They had sleepovers long before we started dating. It's fascinating how everything just worked out. Our children accepted each other and when we announced our intentions, they celebrated and said, "*We're* getting married! *We're* getting married!" There were adjustments because Jack's standard for behavior and my rules were a bit different, so our children had to learn some new rules for behavior. Truth be told, however, all our children are as close to both of us as if we were their natural parents. God has been good to us in that area and we have had few problems.

Jack already mentioned that church was a non-negotiable for me. I encourage all women to have a faith standard and the bar needs to be set high. I know because it's by

God's design that your man will reach up to you if you set the standard. Sex was for later; church was first.

There you have our stories. We hope they will help you relate to us as we walk you through the steps for a successful marriage for the modern couple. There isn't much we haven't seen or heard, and we love to teach and see couples thrive. We invite you, therefore, to walk through these pages with us and allow us to share our journey and lessons we have learned with you. Let's get started in the next few chapters with the foundation for all good marriages and relationships, and that is the practice and hard work of good communication.

CHAPTER 3

COMMUNICATING WITH YOUR PARTNER

As we get started, we want to ask you to consider the question, "What is communication?" For us, it is a purposeful exchange of information between two or more participants, and there is no more important activity to a successful marriage. As you have reflected on "What is communication?", you may answer like most modern couples do. They say it's talking and listening, listening and talking. Sounds simple, doesn't it? Let's look at a simple example with the emphasis put on different words, and we will see that this communication thing is more complex than we thought:

- WHAT are you doing?
- What ARE you doing?
- What are YOU doing?
- What are you DOING?

Those four statements are what's being said. Now here is what the listener can potentially hear when he or she hears each of those four statements:

- I am being challenged that I am doing the wrong thing because the talker is emphasizing the WHAT.
- The whole tone of the statement implies that I am doing nothing.
- This question seems to imply that I am not taking responsibility for my end of the problem or situation at hand.
- Again, I am being challenged because the speaker believes I am doing a wrong or hurtful thing.

We include this example to indicate that even though you are talking, you communicate in many different ways beyond your words. In fact, even when you're not talking, you're still communicating with one another through body language, facial expression, actions, and posture. When couples tell us that they are having trouble communicating, that generally isn't quite true. They *are* communicating, but either one doesn't like what the other is saying (or not saying), or the message is coming through loud and clear, and the other party is offended, angry, or in the mood to respond in kind that will escalate the tension.

Everything in your relationship feeds off your ability to communicate with one another. Many issues arise through misunderstandings. One of the key points to remember is that you can say something, but your hearer has to be able to recognize and comprehend what you mean if there is to be accurate communication. Someone once said marriage is like two people from different countries getting married. They both have to learn a whole new culture, a new language, and new customs. Let's give you another example of what we mean.

One man came from a family that celebrated a birthday *hour* for their family members. They sat down for a dinner, had a cake, gave some presents, and then moved on. His wife came from a family who celebrated a birthday *month*. They did special things all month for the birthday person. How does this relate to communication? When the wife asked, "How are we going to celebrate my birthday?", the husband thought about a dinner. She thought about a festive month-long series of events. Both parties thought they understood what "birthday celebration" meant, but neither understood it from the other's perspective. It took them a few years to come to grips that what each one assumed was a birthday celebration was not what the partner understood it to be.

When the husband planned the dinner, the wife was disappointed and sulked. When the husband saw her demeanor, he was discouraged and angry, and felt his honest efforts were being rejected and criticized. What was the root of the problem? It was communication! Both assumed they knew what the other meant, but neither really did. Both got offended when their concept of the word "celebration" was rejected and criticized by the other. The only way to resolve this problem is learning how to communicate more effectively.

The Bible, our manual for life, provides some tips on how to communicate. One of the verses speaks to the concept of listening to each other in our relationships. That verse is found in James 1:19, where it states, "So then, my beloved brother, let every man be swift to hear, slow to speak, and slow to wrath." It is of note that we each have one mouth and two ears, which was probably God's way of telling us we need to listen twice as much as we speak. The verse in James emphasizes the need to spend more time listening than speaking, implying that when that doesn't occur, anger is soon to follow.

Many problems stem from the fact that modern couples don't follow that two-to-one rule of thumb for listening and speaking. We find that partners are slow to listen and quick to speak to one another, with the result being a lot of confusion, misunderstandings, and hurt feelings. When we don't listen, we begin to form our response before the other person is finished. Or we assume we know what the other party is going to say, so we interrupt them. One of the skills and habits we teach is to have each party listen to the other until he or she is finished. This isn't a marriage problem, it's a cultural problem, because we have many classes and courses on speaking and not very many on listening.

Therefore, we spend our first sessions teaching people how to hear their partner with the intent to understand, *not* to respond. That training includes recognizing body language and visual clues to let the partner know the other is listening. That means eye-to-eye contact, no checking or fingering cell phones, and no television or computers.

Then we move on to active listening, which means the listener is totally engaged mentally in what the other is saying. One simple technique we teach is to have one partner repeat back to the other partner what he or she just said. This can be as simple as, "I know you would like to go out tonight for pizza, but I think we should go out to have Mexican." Do you see what that statement does? It affirms that one partner heard the other. He or she may not agree, but each heard what the other wanted.

If the issue is more complex, then one partner can paraphrase what the other said and repeat it back to him or her. Then the speaker can say, "Yes, that's what I meant" or "No, that's not it at all." Then the process should start all over again until the one partner feels that he or she has been heard. Famous author Steven Covey called this trait, "seek first to understand, then to be understood." Listening involves making sure you understand another, even if you know up front you will disagree with them. You don't assume anything, however, and hear the other party out. That takes discipline and a commitment to listening with the intent to understand.

We know one pastor who uses a principle whenever couples would come to him for marriage counseling. He knew they were there because of some problem, and each was ready to let him know how the wife or husband was in the wrong and needed to be corrected. He would not let them start by telling their story, however, but would ask one of them at the start, "What is your spouse going to tell me about you when he or she has the chance?" What was the pastor doing? He was ascertaining if the spouse had been listening to his partner's complaints about or challenges with him or her. Then he would ask the other partner the same question: "What is your spouse going to tell me about *you*?"

If she would say, "He's going to say I am possessive and talk too much," sometimes the husband would look over and say, "I didn't think you were hearing me!" Or at times one would say, "She is going to tell you that I am spending too much time at work," and she would respond, "No, I am saying you are giving so much at work that you have nothing left for me!" The pastor was assessing how well each party was listening to the another, and that told him what they had to work on.

Let's be honest. This kind of active listening takes work and time. It is sometimes intense and doesn't happen in one encounter or sitting. Another simple practice that both can use is to ask questions to clarify, and to make sure that those questions are not accusatory or inflammatory in any way. A question like, "What about what your brother said to me at Christmas?" is not the kind of question to which we are referring. It is a question that helps clarify what the other is saying, something like, "So you are saying that you felt like I left you alone at the party and then said insensitive things?" You may totally disagree if he or she says "yes" to that question. Yet, you hold your tongue and continue to work on understanding the message so you can fully understand what the problem is, not what you *think* it is

At times, a third party may be needed to sort through what is really being said, or not being said. Of course, understanding what the other is saying is only part of effective communication. Once the problem or issue is clearly understood, then a resolution needs to be identified, and that can require time and change by one or both parties. If the other person is expressing strong feelings, try to acknowledge them without becoming offended or angry yourself—and that's not always easy to do.

We strongly emphasize listening so we can move on to the next trait for effective communication, and that is being assertive. Communication isn't all about the practice of listening, it's being willing to speak what the other partner needs to hear. Once again, the Bible has something to say about this concept: "Do not let any unwholesome talk come out of your mouths, but only what is helpful for building others up according to their needs, that it may benefit those who listen" (Ephesians 4:29). Let's look more closely at that concept of assertiveness in the next chapter, looking at what it is and is not, and how it enters into a a modern marriage relationship where communication is concerned.

Before we move on, let's review some of the key points from this chapter:

1. Everything in your relationship feeds off your ability to communicate with one another.

2. Communication is more about learning to listen than responding to what is said.

3. Listening is a skill that needs to be developed.

Now let's move on to discuss something that most people never consider to be part of effective communication, and that is the trait of assertiveness.

CHAPTER 4

BEING ASSERTIVE WITHOUT BEING A BULLY

We raised the issue of being assertive as we closed the last chapter, and you may be puzzled as to why we include such a concept in a discussion on effective communication between marriage partners. We alluded to our reason at the end of the last chapter, and we include it because there are times when one or both parties shut down when there is tension as they communicate. They don't want the pain of an argument so they may say nothing when something needs to be said. Something needs to be said, it just needs to be said in the correct way.

Please don't misunderstand. Being assertive is not being mean, angry, or a bully. It simply means that you say what you need to say without holding back. When your partner asks you, "What's wrong?" and you respond, "Nothing," but in reality, you are hurt or bothered, you are not being assertive. You are not giving your partner what he or she needs to hear. You are withholding the truth. Now, you may have to say, "I can't talk about it right now, I'm still processing." Eventually, however, you have to be assertive and speak what's on your mind. When you are assertive, it is for two reasons: You need to say it and your partner needs to hear it so he or she can respond and even improve in their communication skills.

One way that we try to foster assertiveness is by having each person in the relationship compose three wish lists of what he or she would like in life or from their marriage relationship. They don't share the list with each other initially. The purpose is to help whoever may not be assertive to be able to learn some assertiveness skills by thinking about themselves, which some find hard to do. It's vital that you learn to let your partner know how you feel, what you want, and what your desires are, but you can't do that if you won't acknowledge how you feel, don't know what you want, or don't believe your desires are worthy of consideration. After the partners have made their list, we bring the couples back together and have them discuss what they have written.

When they write out their list, here are the rules. One, both must use the word "I." We don't allow one to say, "My wish is for you to clean the house more." Rather, it would be stated, "I wish to have a house that is more in order." By focusing on me or I, the individual is not attacking the other, but speaking only in the first person, expressing their wishes and desires. Then we have them describe just what their wish looks like, how it makes them feel, and what they would like to see as the final result. The listener's job is to repeat what he or she has heard, summarize it, and then repeat it back to the other party so that person knows he or she was understood. After that, they switch roles and the speaker becomes the listener.

If you love your partner, you will not withhold the truth from him or her. You must be willing to share your needs and your perspective. With good listening habits, you may hear a perspective from your partner that you had not considered, for example, when you became worried or upset, but it all starts with being willing to put yourself out there and be vulnerable.

During our seminars, we try to do some fun things to teach communication principles. Here is one we do that you can try in the comfort of your own home. It's called, "Let's draw a house." We have couples sit next to each other and they are not permitted to speak. We then put a sheet of paper in front of them. We ask the couples to join hands holding one pen or pencil and direct them to draw their dream house, without saying anything. We have found that to be a remarkable tool to find out who is the dominant one in the relationship. Oftentimes, it's a lot of fun because they're laughing while they do it. We also like this exercise because it teaches them the power of nonverbal communication.

Another activity is to have the couples look at a picture and describe what each one sees. For instance, we use one picture of a young person who is sitting on a railroad track looking off in the distance. When the couples start describing what they see, usually both have a totally different perspective with unique insight. We use this to help couples listen to one another and to realize that what each sees is not wrong, it is simply different. Then we use some of the three-dimensional pictures where there is a 3-D picture embedded in a seemingly meaningless picture design.

What one sees, the other may not see it for quite a while, if ever. We use that to teach the couples that it's not a matter of effort, or desire, or intelligence, or spirituality to perceive what another finds common knowledge. One can't see because it's simply more difficult for him or her to see the hidden pattern. It will take more time, and the one isn't being stubborn or resistant to what the other is saying or seeing. He or she just cannot see it for whatever reason.

We also use a children's game where you have to put the pieces into the ball through the hole in the ball that matches the shape of the piece being inserted. That's pretty simple. We time how quickly one of the partners can put the pieces in the ball, and it's usually about 30 seconds. Then we have them do it together, and it takes about 10 seconds. That gives them a vision for how effective it can be if they work together, and it all starts with listening. If each partner can learn to listen to the other's insight, they can solve problems more quickly and see opportunities more quickly as well. It can be a lot of fun.

We have another exercise called "Where do you see yourself in five years?" While each party is answering that question for themselves, they are also answering it for each other. The wife may be thinking of going back to school or moving on in her career, but her husband is thinking that he wants her to stop and have a family. Now we have an issue that has been identified and needs to be discussed. That will require both parties to listen, ask questions, give feedback, and come to a clear understanding of where the other is and why. And the entire process requires assertiveness—the willingness for each party to speak the truth as he or she sees it.

Finally, we also recommend that modern couples watch TV shows or sitcoms, something like the show that was on a few years ago, *Everybody Loves Raymond*. We give them an assignment, and then we ask them to come back to the next session and critique the show from a communication perspective. What did you see that was effective communication? How did they communicate? What did they do wrong? What could they have said and done differently? Then at the end of it, we ask them to review what each party saw and determine how it applies to their relationship.

Of course, we cannot finish a discussion on communication without looking at speech and the power of our words. The Bible has some important and painful reminders about the power of words: "The tongue has the power of life and death, and those who love it will eat its fruit" (Proverbs 18:21). We have much to say on this topic, so let's move on to the next chapter that will be totally devoted to that topic.

So what have we learned about being assertive in this chapter?

1. Being assertive is not being mean, angry, or a bully. It simply means that you say what you need to say without holding back.

2. If you love your partner, you will not withhold the truth from him or her.

3. Being assertive requires courage both to speak and to listen.

Next, we will look at what most people consider to be the essence of communication, and that is spoken words, the source of much marital conflict.

CHAPTER 5

WATCH YOUR WORDS

Many of us have been trained from a young age to express ourselves, and social media has only added to that emphasis, providing an opportunity to share with the world our feelings, opinions, and perspective. Have you ever watched a touchdown celebration in a professional football game? Sometimes it gets out of hand in self-expression, because it becomes selfish. Once you're a couple, it's not only *I*, it's also *we*. If you take an *I* view of everything, you are leaving out a key part of a relationship and your communication can become selfish, just like those end zone celebrations. We have to be careful with self-expression and always wanting things go the way we want them to go. According to the Bible, when you're married, you become one flesh. So the "I" is gone and we must concentrate on the "we."

Paul wrote in Philippians 2:3-4, "Do nothing out of selfish ambition or vain conceit. Rather, in humility value others above yourselves, not looking to your own interests but each of you to the interests of the others." As Paul was writing this, he wasn't specifically speaking to married people, but rather describing a philosophy that applied to all life situations, which includes married people and folks who are single. Paul is saying to look out for others as much or more than we look out for ourselves.

Psalm 141:3 says, "Take control of what I say, O' Lord. And keep my lips sealed." It's interesting that 3,100 years ago, David was addressing the problem of saying the wrong thing at the wrong time, and was asking God's help to keep from doing it! In another psalm, the writer wrote, "May the words of my mouth and meditation of my heart be acceptable in thy sight, O Lord, my strength and my redeemer." Obviously, David didn't mean that he wanted his lips permanently sewn up. He just wanted to make sure he was pleasing God with what he said. It's not possible to go through life without communicating. Even when you don't say anything, you may be saying or communicating a lot.

Therefore, the Bible warns us to be slow to speak or not to speak at all. When you are slow to speak, it means you are considering what you will say before you say it. We need to understand that the volume of words you are using is not important. What's important is what you say, how you say it, the intent behind it, and the tone that you use. If you want to communicate effectively, no matter how many words you use, the hearer must receive and understand or it's a waste of time. You want to be effective in your communicating, and not just say what's on your mind. For that to happen, you must pay attention so you can help the other person comprehend what you say.

That being said, why is it that we can talk the worst to those whom we love the most and are closest to us? In our marriage relationships and in our families, our words should always be seasoned with grace that includes respect for the other person's own thoughts and feelings as Paul wrote in Colossians 4:6: "Let your speech always be with grace, seasoned with salt, that you may know how to answer each one." When something is seasoned with hot pepper, it may not taste good to anyone else. If you are the cook, you must not only consider your taste, but also the taste of others. The same is true for communication. You may use words that seem appropriate to you but those words may be offensive to others. What will you do? Keep serving up dishes of words that no one else wants to consume?

It may feel good to get your licks in with sharp words that are intended to cut, fashioned to win an argument, or shut your partner down. When you do that, however, what have you gained? What is the end result? We don't want to be crude, but that whole process of speaking your mind with no regard to the implications is kind of like a baby relieving itself in its bathwater. It may feel good at the moment, but then the baby has to sit in it. When you insult or offend your spouse, it may feel good at the moment, but then you have to live in the atmosphere of tension and anger that you helped create! That is not only counterproductive to a healthy relationship, it is also not in your own best personal interests.

As we said, the Bible has plenty to say about communication. While Philippians 4:8 is not specifically about words, it does speak to a communications philosophy that each couple should adopt when it comes to their relationship in general: "Finally, brothers and sisters, whatever is true, whatever is noble, whatever is right, whatever is pure, whatever is lovely, whatever is admirable—if anything is excellent or praiseworthy— think about such things."
Notice the list of things to consider. What in our relationship is true and noble? What and how do I communicate? Am I sarcastic? Are my words sharp and cutting? Or is what I say true and honorable? This verse provides objectives that if each modern couple followed, it would create a more conducive environment for a healthy relationship through godly communication.

How often have you spent time rehearsing how you were going to rip into your partner? If you actually think and strategize about what you want to say and how you want to say it, you have less of an opportunity to dwell on some of the of the wrong things to say. Before you speak, you will want to consider, as best you can, what's going to come out of your mouth so you don't have a minute or a lifetime of regret over what you said—or what you didn't say.

Couples have a wonderful opportunity to encourage and build the other partner up through what they say. You don't want to rehearse only what you are going to say in a heated moment, but you want to rehearse and then speak positive things, things that will uplift and make your partner's day. This can be through a poem you write, or a greeting card you buy and tuck under his or her pillow, or place in his or her briefcase. It may be the text message you send at various times throughout the day, saying that you are thinking about your partner. Yes, we try to teach modern couples that it's not just what we say but what goes unsaid that has tragic or unfortunate consequences.

We also discuss under communication the importance of communicating love through special events. Jack will often talk to the men about continuing to date their wives after the courting is over. Helen reminds women that they also have a responsibility to plan special times with their husbands, even if it is a night at home watching a special movie. There are also plenty of inexpensive places where a couple can go for a lunch or dinner date.

Whatever you did to bring you to the point where you wanted to spend the rest of your life with this person, you should continue to do after you are married. That's part of communication! You are saying through actions and perhaps words, "I would marry you all over again! I love you and really enjoy spending time with you, just you!" Develop a time when you're praying for the well-being of your mate, that he or she will have a great day. Pray for their work experience, and everything that concerns their world of work or family. Give thanks for them and let them know you thank God for them.

When you enter into a prolonged relationship, you tend to forget about the little things you both like to do. If you sent flowers while you were dating, send flowers now. That's a good way to communicate without saying a word. When you wake up in the morning, the first thing you should say to your wife or mate is, "Good morning, honey. I love you." It can be very short and sweet, but can have a powerful impact, especially when the mate knows it's heartfelt. Often after they start having problems or conflicts, couples then resort back to those things to try and patch things up and end the tension. That may work, but it should not be a technique, it should be a lifestyle that happens before, during, and after a tense time or dispute.

When you speak kind, gracious words, it's almost like putting money in the bank for a time when it's needed. Couples will be able to withdraw from that account in times of trouble, and it will go a long way towards soothing difficult times. You'll be able to work through them faster, because you'll really know how your mate is feeling and have his or her best interests at heart.

You may communicate your love and commitment by doing something outside of your normal role or duties. If you never serve as the dishwasher, load it and empty it. If you never clean the front yard, clean off the lawn. Whatever it is that's *not* your normal role, do it and watch how effective that is in your communication and relationship with your spouse. You are saying, "I love you so much, I am willing to do the things I don't like or enjoy if it will make you happy." Again, you will be communicating but without words.

There are plenty of communication pitfalls, some of which we have already covered. Don't ever use profanity or offensive accusations or insults. The obvious ones are things like, "You are fat" or "You're too skinny" or "You're acting like your mother or father." Proverbs 15:1-2 says, "A soft answer turns away wrath, but a harsh word stirs up anger. The tongue of the wise uses knowledge lightly. But the mouth of fools pours forth foolishness." When we speak softly as Proverbs 15:1 advises, we can defuse negative feelings and promote a positive relationship. We teach couples that they don't have to yell to make their point. It's not the loudness that gets through, it's the love that gets through.

Proverbs 25:11-12 reminds us that "A word fitly spoken is like apples of gold in settings of silver. Like an earring of gold and ornament of fine gold is a wise rebuke to an obedient ear." Ephesians 4:15 states, "But speaking the truth in love, may grow up in all things in to him who is the head, Christ." We ultimately want to lead people back to their obligations to Christ. If He's the center of their relationships, they will be successful no matter what they go through because they each will do what God wants them to do regardless of their partner's response. After 26 years of marriage, which included bankruptcies and places we thought would wipe us out completely, we're much stronger because we kept Christ at the center of what we did and how we responded to circumstances and to one another.

We also teach modern couples to remember and utilize five words, and those five words are: "I'm sorry" and "I forgive you." Both parties at some point in the relationship are going to cause a misunderstanding and be less than perfect. When that happens, the offending party needs to say, "I'm sorry I hurt your feelings" or "I'm sorry I didn't understand. Please forgive me." It's then important for the offended party to say "I forgive you," because no relationship can thrive while someone is holding a grudge.

The Bible lets us know that to be forgiven, we have to forgive. When we say we forgive, then we must truly forgive. Otherwise, the next time an argument comes up, whether in two weeks or two years, we can begin rehash the same thing because there was no forgiveness extended. When you forgive, once it's in the past, it stays in the past. If you have forgiven your partner, don't bring it up again. Take it out of your mind as best you can and move on.

One of the things one of our trainers pointed out is that they don't say "I'm sorry, but…" in their family. That only ends up giving everyone a "sorry butt." There are a lot of sorry butts in many households. When someone says, "I'm sorry I hurt you, *but* if your mother wouldn't have done that, then I would not have done what I did." That person may be sorry, but they are using someone else as an excuse for his or her bad behavior. There is a big difference between being sorry as opposed to asking for forgiveness. You can be sorry for the consequences, but not be sorry for what you did. Asking forgiveness requires humility and putting pride aside. You have to acknowledge that you were wrong, regardless of whether or not your partner recognizes and confesses any wrong on his or her part.

There is so still more to cover where communication is concerned, but let's end this chapter by saying that we also have the couples complete a couple's assessment that gives them more information about one another's personality to help in the communication process. One partner may be naturally less talkative; one much more prone to remember details and thus less likely to forgive; one may find it almost impossible to say he or she was wrong. All this is important to know and can help or hinder communication. At the end of this book, we share with you where you can find this assessment, but we advise you that the assessment is much more effective when you have another couple or individual helping walk you through the results so you can apply them.

Do you think we have covered it all where communication is concerned? The answer is "not yet!" We have a bit more to say in the final chapter before we move on to the topic of roles and responsibilities. Let's go there now, and talk a bit more about communicating through actions and attitudes.

Have you learned something about speech and words in the chapter? As we close, here are a few things to keep in mind:

1. The Bible warns us to be slow to speak or not to speak at all.

2. Your words can either build up or tear down, so make every effort to build your partner up by choosing your words carefully.

3. There is a difference between saying, "I'm sorry," and "Forgive me." The goal in a relationship is not to explain why you did something wrong, but to seek forgiveness for saying or doing wrong.

We are not quite ready to move on from communication, for there is one more chapter we need to include to help you enhance your ability to communicate. Let's go there now.

CHAPTER 6

MORE IS BETTER

We usually spend more time on communication than anything else (yes, even more than sex), and we do this because communication is the most important skill we can have in a relationship. Since it is the most important, it's also the number one cause of problems in a relationship. Let's not be in too much of a hurry, and spend a little more time on this important skill.

We saw a survey recently that stated 76% of modern couples wished their partner was more willing to share his or her feelings. Another 65% said that their partner did not understand or know how to accept their partner's feelings. A lot of times, that happens because individuals fear ridicule, and also because some have never learned how to talk about themselves or their feelings! As difficult as it may be for some, it's imperative that couples learn to share their feelings. One of the skills we facilitate in our classes is showing how couples can request what they need from their partner and not be afraid of rejection. We know sometimes people have difficulty asking their partner for what they want or need, which gets back to the topic of assertiveness that we covered earlier.

There are a few of Bible verses that help with this practice. One is Proverbs 20:5, which states, "The purposes of a person's heart are deep waters, but one who has insight draws them out." This indicates that each spouse needs to become skilled in helping his or her partner express what is really in his or her heart because those feelings can be very deep waters. Often, one partner or the other will refuse to discuss how he or she feels. That partner will claim nothing is wrong, when there are all kinds of feelings and issues with which he or she needs to deal with and discuss. Both partners need to learn how to be open and discuss how they feel, and both need to become adept at providing an environment where that can take place.

The first thing we teach is for people to share about themselves and to avoid criticizing their partner. Here is what we teach them *not* to say and do: "When you don't take out the trash, you are being lazy and I've had enough of it." The better thing to say is, "When you don't take out the trash, it upsets me and causes me to feel that I am alone in caring for the house." Do you see the difference?

Going back to what we discussed in Chapter 3, the partner on the receiving end should summarize what he or she heard: "So you are saying that it upsets you when I don't take out the trash. Do you feel it is disrespectful and puts more pressure on you?" Right there is a breakthrough of sorts. One partner shared feelings and the other listened and gave feedback to indicate he or she has heard. What's especially helpful is that a time is set aside to talk about the feelings of both parties where no one is defensive or accusatory. We want couples to communicate and talk to each other, because when they are not talking, they are still communicating! Even when you're quiet, you're communicating something.

When one partner tells the other he or she should *not* feel like they do, it is communicating that there is something defective or wrong with the partner and his or her feelings. Now, that feeling partner may in reality be too sensitive or have an anger problem, and that may need to be changed or adjusted. But when the offended partner claims that their spouse should not feel that way, it doesn't leave the offending party many options. They must either ignore how they feel, or they can hold on to how they feel because they haven't found a reason *not* to feel that way. Therefore, no progress or growth takes place on either partner's part.

As we stated earlier, if a special time can be established to talk, then it's time that is solely devoted to communication. There should be no TV or cellphones. It's often helpful to start out sharing the good qualities you see in each other, and then move on from there. You may want to set a time limit on how long you will talk, but the more skilled you become at this, the less likely it is that you will want to end a really good session!

Then there is a verse in 1 Peter 3:7 that speaks to the husbands and says, "Husbands, in the same way be considerate as you live with your wives, and treat them with respect as the weaker partner and as heirs with you of the gracious gift of life, so that nothing will hinder your prayers." The word that is so important for both partners is to be "considerate." Lest you think we are picking on the husbands, this is what it says in Ephesians 5:33: "However, each one of you also must love his wife as he loves himself, and the wife must respect her husband." The key element in that verse for the wife is respect. If you are being considerate and have respect for one another, it will go a long way toward improving your ability to communicate. That means you will be considerate of and have respect for your partner's feelings.

One of the things that can be difficult for some modern couples to understand is that intimacy and foreplay don't start in the bedroom. They start when you wake up in the morning. One of the things we talk about to enhance intimacy is to compliment your partner as often as possible. By complimenting your partner, you create a closeness and a feeling of respect and admiration. When partners can sincerely give a compliment to each other, they have less problems throughout the day. We also recommend that partners, at least once a week, have a date night or something to that effect. If you have children, get a babysitter. You must have time to spend together and bond.

The word intimacy can loosely be described as *knowing* someone in the Hebrew language. You don't get to know people and become familiar with the intimate things in a relationship until you can communicate them—one shares while the other one listens.

When we talk about developing a more personal, intimate relationship, we make three other recommendations. The first is to write one another notes. Be light-hearted with some of the stuff you write. It doesn't have to be a long letter. Maybe you leave a note if your spouse stays in bed after you leave for work. Maybe you can put a little sticky note in his or her car or put something on the kitchen counter or in a briefcase. I'm [Helen] the kind of person who likes that.

Second, we talk about doing things together. Couples can take a class together, something that interests them both, but they must do it together. These are things that develop more conversations and give them something to talk about to one another. If you can't afford a date night, be a little more creative and have a cheap date night. How does a cheap date night look? It might be hot dog night when you cook them over an open fire or on the grill. It can be a movie that's on TV with no kids around. Maybe it's a game of Scrabble or a playing card tournament.

Third, establish fun traditions together, things that mean something special to the two of you. One of our traditions is birthday helium balloons because they aren't expensive and we can always afford them. The idea is that as long as the balloons are floating, the recipient is celebrated and made to feel special. Another example of a tradition may be a vacation, an annual drive to view autumn leaves changing, a Friday night trip to the mall, a game the two of you play that *only* the two of you play together—never with anyone else. All those things develop conversations. We recommend that you do anything that keeps you talking. Do not stop talking to each other because when you do, it's dangerous for your relationship.

When you have a date night, do what your partner likes to do. You can alternate between the two of you so that each partner gets a chance to choose the activity. Sometimes I [Jack] may not necessarily want to go to the opera, but I know if that's something that really pleases Helen, I can bank some big points into our relationship account by going to the opera. You may even be surprised how much you enjoy it, maybe not necessarily the event itself, but just being with your partner and watching him or her enjoy themselves.

When we don't communicate properly or regularly, we tend to make assumptions. We assume we know our partner's motives, and we may indeed know. More often than not, however, we don't know, and we expend and waste a lot of emotional energy by getting upset over what we assumed was going on. You don't want to get into the habit of making assumptions about your partner. You want to ask, but when you do, you have to be the kind of person who is willing to allow your partner to ask you. If you want your partner to listen to you, then you have to listen to them. There is a mutuality that must take place or else the relationship becomes one-sided.

It helps to know your communication style, and yes, you do have one. You may be an avoider, because if that's the way you are, then that's the way you will [not] communicate. And your partner needs to know what your style is. My [Helen] husband is much more assertive now, but he grew into that. When we first got married, he was more introverted and laid back, and really could not say what he was feeling. He could be unhappy about something but not say anything.

And I [Helen], being so gregarious and outgoing, would completely overlook it. It was not intentional; I just didn't see it. I would be on to the next thing and he would be stewing and brooding over what had happened. We needed to be aware of our styles. I would come back around and discover I had really done something that was not to his liking, so I needed to go back and revisit that, apologize, and acknowledge that I didn't realize I did that—or that what I did upset him. I had to work on my sensitivity. It's not easy and an overnight thing.

There is a one scenario when partners are communicating well, and that's when they are arguing. Then anger provides the incentive and motivation to air it all out, but often the argument can do more harm than good. The idea is that the couple learns to enjoy the effects of an argument without actually having one! More on that will come up later when we address conflict resolution. Yet the real key is to learn—and it can be learned—to communicate difficult, emotionally-charged things without losing one's temper.

When you communicate, you have to be honest. You can't be misleading. Your goal is not to win the argument or get your way. The goal is for your partner to understand you and you her (or him). When a man and woman have been together for any length of time, they discover what buttons to push that get a rise out of their partner. The bottom line isn't about being right; the goal is resolving the issue. A lot of times we'll continue arguments just to prove we were right, and that can cause more problems than it is worth. Your main goal should be having a relationship that's functional and growing. There are times where even though in your mind you *think* you're right, weigh all the issues before making that final push to prove you are right.

The book of Proverbs has a lot to say about communication between people, but the principles certainly apply to modern couples. Let's look at some of the wisdom we can find in that book.

- Proverbs 18:13 states, "To answer before listening is folly and a shame." We have repeatedly emphasized the need for good listening skills, and this verse endorses that discipline.

- Proverbs 17:1 says, "Better a dry crust with peace and quiet than a house full of feasting, with strife." While there are some who like the argument technique for communication, we are not among them. This verse says it's better to be poor than to be wealthy where a lot of fussing and fighting is going on. (You may disagree, but let's not argue with the Bible!)

- Proverbs 13:17 teaches that "a wicked messenger falls into trouble, but a trustworthy envoy brings healing." Our goal as partners should always be to bring healing and not cause trouble or pain through our communication techniques.

One of the most difficult things for couples to do is to talk about sex and to learn how to ask for what one likes or doesn't like, what one wants, what one needs, and how one feels, and to be able to speak about that. There are still many taboos, especially in the Christian or religious community, when it comes to an open discussion about sex. Those taboos weren't established by God, because God created sex. [Helen: And people always gasp when Jack shares the fact that God created sex.]

God did indeed institute sex, not just to procreate, but to give pleasure. Over time, a false morality attached stigmas to sex, and pressured couples not to talk about it. The church bears a lot of responsibility for allowing that to happen, because very few churches ever address the issue of sex. They keep it on a back burner when the church should be the hub, not just of the religious and spiritual life, but the physical life as well—mind, body and soul. Another problem is that the media has glamorized sex, portraying it as something that is to be accompanied by fireworks and multiple orgasms. Any experienced married couple can tell you that sex is not always something that meets both the expectations of both parties. Fatigue, career pressures, problems with the children, physical illnesses, disagreements, and moods can make sex difficult to have let alone enjoy.

When couples wait until they get to bed to talk about sex, that can be a problem. We heard a couple describe how they had a small decorative box on their nightstand. When one partner was interested in having sex that night, he or she would raise the top. If the top stayed up when they got to bed, things were on. If the top went down, however, it wasn't going to happen that day. That was a form of communication, but something they had agreed to and worked on. A man has to work to understand the physiology of the woman and the rhythms of her month so that he is not disappointed when he plans a big night but she is on the "physically unable to perform" list. The couple found the box helped establish the mood of the moment.

Someone once wrote a book that stated sex starts in the kitchen. What he meant by that is couples start intimacy when they help with the dishes or by holding a conversation at the dinner table. If you wait for sex to start in the bedroom, that's where a lot of the miscommunication, frustration, and anger can occur. One partner thought something was going to happen and then he or she was thwarted and frustrated. Then the tone can become sharp and accusatory. That's another aspect of communication of which you need to be aware: Avoid exaggeration. Saying something like, "You are *never* interested in having sex" or "You want to have sex *every* night" may not truthful. In reality, it was only once or twice. When you exaggerate to make your point and win the argument, you're not really being truthful and the person can hear that and dismiss it as irrelevant because it's exaggerated.

As difficult as it is to talk about sex, it's almost as difficult for some modern couples to pray together. I [Jack] recently pointed out to my church that people would never know if Helen and I had an argument on the way to church by how we relate to one another once we get to church. We've made a pact that no matter how much we disagree on whatever issue, once we get to the church, we are going to worship and pray together and do whatever we can to allow the Holy Spirit to minister to us as individuals. We chuckle because we have never carried our baggage into the church and never brought it up again after church. It's vitally important that believers learn how to pray together because prayer is a form of communicating. We are communicating with the One who can help us solve our problems. When we're praying, we're taking the focus off the pain of the issue and our personal disappointments, and understanding what God has for each of us in regards to the other.

Jonah was in the belly of the whale, and he prayed. He talked about the problems he had first. He said he was in trouble and whatever else he said, he had a lot of issues. The Bible tells us that he gave a sacrifice of thanksgiving to the Lord and as soon as that happened, the whale spat him out. If you can pray together, it's the first step toward getting your problems solved. If you can pray together and focus on the resolution as opposed to all of the issues, you stand a better chance of getting your problems solved.

We hope we have communicated how important communication is! If couples can learn to listen, give feedback, ask good questions, and use their words to heal and build up instead of hurt and tear down, then they will be well on their way to having a healthy and growing relationship. Perhaps one more verse from the Bible would help here. Jesus said, "Whoever wants to be my disciple must deny themselves and take up their cross daily and follow me" (Luke 9:23).

Good communication is an opportunity for each partner to pick up his or her cross and follow Jesus. When your point of view is ignored, it's time to pick up your cross and do what's best for your partner. When you listen and listen, and don't feel like your partner reciprocates, it's time to pick up your cross. When you listen when you want to speak, when you share your feelings and they are misunderstood, when you encourage and there is no encouragement in return, they are all opportunities to pick up your cross. That doesn't mean you can't share how you feel or the disappointment you have, but it does mean that you won't retaliate pitch a fit when things don't go your way. Yes, when those things happen, it indicates that your relationship needs some work, but it also provides a wonderful opportunity to love unconditionally.

What did we learn in this chapter? Here are a few of the highlights:

1. It's imperative that couples learn to share their feelings.

2. Sex is God's will (for married couples), but sex can be a difficult topic where communication is concerned.

3. The Bible has many helpful tips to enhance communication in a marriage. You would do well to study what it has to say.

It's time to move on, so in our next section, let's examine the issue of roles and responsibilities and how those are managed and identified in any married relationship. Be mindful, however, that we will refer back to the concepts we have discussed in these communication chapters, so make sure you have a good grasp of what we have discussed before you move on!

CHAPTER 7

ROLES AND RESPONSIBILITIES

In every culture, there are stereotypes that are imposed on each relationship concerning various roles and responsibilities. Sometimes subcultures impose those roles and responsibilities even when the dominant culture does not. In other words, there are always pressures on every modern couple to conform to certain standards of what the man and what the woman "should" be doing as they live out their relationship. Couples must be able to clearly define what each partner's expectations are for those responsibilities in the context of their unique relationship. As this evolves, roles in one relationship are going to be very different than another, and those duties and roles may change over time.

Traditionally in Western cultures, the wife has been the chief homemaker. If she chooses to work, the couple must address who does the things she was expected to do to keep a household. We found in our role with The Marriage Works that many non-traditional roles were being displayed among the variety of men and women with whom we worked. For instance, in one household, the husband did all the cooking and housework. Both partners worked, but he still took care of all of that. We are not advocating for that scenario, we just recommend that the roles and responsibilities be clearly defined and understood. We also try to have couples be flexible enough for roles and responsibilities to change. If you're in a relationship for any length of time, roles will tend to morph, for a number of reasons. One of them might be the health of one of the partners. That's why we say the roles should be clearly defined and redefined, if need be, on a regular basis.

If I'm {Jack] the one who has the most skill at budgeting, then I should be the one balancing the checkbook. If one of the partners leans more towards maintaining the house, then he or she should do that. If you have a male-dominated relationship, that means he is going to make the bulk of the decisions. The decisions the wife makes are few and far between, and those decisions have to go through a screening process with the husband before the couple makes a move. If you can delineate the roles and responsibilities more equally, then both parties will have a say in the roles for that relationship.

As we mentioned earlier, a marriage takes place between two people from completely different family cultures (and sometimes ethnic or national cultures) that are sometimes from completely different planets or from rival universes! Both parties grew up with family traditions and cultures, and sometimes those cultures were reinforced by church or whatever part of the country where the partner grew up. Our point is that each partner has traditions and those traditions can be considered "sacred," but they should not be. It's permissible, in fact advisable, to establish a new family culture for each couple that is formed.

For example, let's say that one spouse's family went to eat at Grandma's house every Sunday. It's now up to the couple to determine if they will continue that tradition or start a new one. Grandma may pitch a fit if they change the tradition, but that is none of Grandma's business! Perhaps another spouse opened their family's Christmas gifts on Christmas Eve. That tradition isn't sacred; the new family unit may wish to change it and start a new tradition.

The same holds true for roles and responsibilities. Maybe Mother always handled the finances in one partner's family, but that isn't necessarily how it should be with her children's families. Yet one partner can insist that's the way it *has* to be. We advocate for more of a strengths-based approach. Whoever has the gift and enjoys handling the finances should do so. Or maybe the responsibility should rotate every five years. Perhaps the couple should hire an accountant and let him or her handle almost all the financial oversight with their input.

Just because we are advocating for clarity of roles and expectations does not mean that either partner becomes the czar of that particular area. Once the roles are set, the couple needs to read Chapters 3 through 6 about communication again. Both the man and woman need to respect the boundaries for each area, but at the same time should solicit feedback from his or her partner about that area, like cooking, finances, vacations, major purchases, and the like.

One area that we cover and get a lot of questions about is the issue of the wife submitting to her husband, for this is a role that God instructs her to assume as a wife. Let's look at what the Bible has to say about that role and responsibility:

- Wives, submit yourselves to your own husbands as you do to the Lord. For the husband is the head of the wife as Christ is the head of the church, his body, of which he is the Savior. Now as the church submits to Christ, so also wives should submit to their husbands in everything (Ephesians 5:22-24).

- Wives, submit yourselves to your husbands, as is fitting in the Lord (Colossians 3:28).

- Wives, in the same way submit yourselves to your own husbands so that, if any of them do not believe the word, they may be won over without words by the behavior of their wives, when they see the purity and reverence of your lives (1 Peter 3:1-2).

Let's talk first about what these verses do *not* mean. The man is not to be the tyrant or dictator of the house. We have all heard stories, if we have been around churches long enough, of husbands who have a disagreement with their wives and try to end it by commanding their wives to "submit!" That's missing the point entirely. There is a short phrase in one of those passages that says: "[submit] as unto the Lord." Does God lord it over those whom He asks to submit? Isn't that submission based on love, honor, and respectful behavior? If the husband is godly, and that's a big *if*, and is seeking to be a better Christian and better man, then he would not take advantage of some of things that were put in place and established by God. The husband is the head, but he is the head of equals. Any husband who understands what godly submission is will not order or command his wife to submit. We will study his godly responsibility next, but for now let's look at what those verses *do* mean for the wife.

God has established an order for every household, and that order requires the wife to submit to the husband's authority. Submission is not popular in today's culture, especially in Western culture where individualism is so highly honored. Yet God is a God of order and He established the order for households as it is described. The husband is to create an environment of openness and love, and the wife is to establish an environment of honor and respect.

If we go back to what we learned in the communications chapters, we understand that submission is not being quiet, unseen, and unheard. There are some cultures where the women not only act like that, they dress like that. They are not to be seen as an individual and only have an identity with their husband or male family figure. We reject that as totally contrary to the Christian, biblical view. In fact, this is what Peter went on to say in the passage we quoted above:

> Your beauty should not come from outward adornment, such as elaborate hairstyles and the wearing of gold jewelry or fine clothes. Rather, it should be that of your inner self, the unfading beauty of a gentle and quiet spirit, which is of great worth in God's sight. For this is the way the holy women of the past who put their hope in God used to adorn themselves. They submitted themselves to their own husbands, like Sarah, who obeyed Abraham and called him her lord. You are her daughters if you do what is right and do not give way to fear (1 Peter 3:2-6).

Notice that a godly wife is *not* to rely on outward adornment, but the Bible does not forbid the outward adornment altogether. What the Bible is more interested in is the heart, and a woman's heart is to be submissive first and foremost to the Lord, and then to the role God designed her to play in her family. If she has poured her heart out to her husband and is convinced that her husband has heard her and respects her thoughts and loves her, then that wife is obligated to abide by the decisions her husband makes.

Before the verses directed toward the wife in Ephesians 5, there is one little verse that helps put the submission issue in proper perspective. It states, "Submit to one another out of reverence for Christ" (Ephesians 5:21). The husband and wife mutually submit to the Lord and His commands, but then they also submit to one another's strengths.

If a wife is over the kitchen, then the husband submits to how she runs the kitchen. He doesn't have to make the decisions about what glasses or dishes she chooses. Yet the wife will consult the husband to see what his choices and preferences are. Both are mutually submitting to one another.

If the husband handles the investments, then he will get input from his wife and do everything he can to consider and carry out her preferences. Do you see how no one should be hung up on who is in charge? Both are focusing on bringing God's wisdom to their respective duties while they love, respect, and listen to their partner.

We have a pastor friend who told that his wife can go a long time *without* making a decision. She's really comfortable with that role. He, on the other hand, wants to make decisions every day. When no decision needs to be made, he has learned to submit to her gift and strength. But if a decision needs to be made quickly, his wife knows he is more comfortable making that kind of decision with her input. And if it's the "wrong" decision, they have learned to live with it because it needed to be made quickly, and quick decisions aren't always the best. The pastor also told us he had to learn that he is not the only one who is permitted to make a mistake in their marriage. Sometimes he errs in quick decisions and sometimes his wife errs in drawn out decisions. In both instances, it's usually not the end of the world.

There are roles that both partners play with the children as well. Sometimes one partner is the disciplinarian, and the other one is the fun parent. The fun parent often wants to circumvent discipline and the disciplinarian wants to set rules around everything. If the couple can learn that neither is wrong but simply represents two different but complementary styles, then they can determine the *need* at the moment—discipline or fun—and rely on the partner who has the necessary tendency to lead the way.

After all, it is the Lord who gives gifts and talents. When someone has a strength, that also means they have a weakness. Many modern couples get confused because when they first met, they reported to anyone who would listen, "Oh, we have so much in common" and they did. They had their values in common—they love family, exercise, and belong to the same political party and grew up in the same denomination. They concluded that they were made for each other.

Then when they start to relate on a long-term basis, they find out the differing tendencies and gifts they have, which are usually quite opposite of one another. They then can begin to think, "I made a mistake! This person isn't who I thought he or she was!" That's not really the case, for they didn't really *know* the other person as well as they thought. What's more, life circumstances had not yet revealed who he or she was. It wasn't until they encountered financial troubles that the husband or wife saw how the spouse responded under pressure. It wasn't until their child brought home a D on his or her report card that they discovered who was the disciplinarian.

In fact, we inform couples that God brings your opposite to you. He is the one who is looking to complement your weaknesses with your partner's strengths and vice versa. When you see those things emerge, it is a surprise to you but not to the Lord. He knew those differences were there, and what's more, He set them up! One friend likes to tell couples, "When two players play the same position well on any sports team, someone is going to get traded. Good teams build on diversity. The same is true for married couples. Don't run from your differences; embrace them!"

In our seminars, we spend some time having the men and women examine their various roles to see if they are "strength-based." Did those roles emerge or were they a conscious decision of who would do what? Were they based on family or church traditions or were they made based on what's in each household's best interests? We had one couple whose husband handled the finances because that is the way they thought it should be done. It turns out, even though he has a master's degree in economics, that the wife is the better household financial manager. Changing the roles caused their household finances to change for the better. The wife handles the finances with her husband's input, but he is learning to rely on her skill that is much better than his proved to be.

Let's summarize our discussion of roles and responsibilities from this chapter:

1. Couples must work to clearly define what each partner's expectations are for those responsibilities in the context of their unique relationship

2. Roles and responsibilities should be based not on tradition or ideals, but on the strengths and weaknesses of each partner.

3. Roles will change over time as the people in the relationship and the life circumstances all change.

Closely related to the issue of roles and responsibilities is something that we have alluded to in this chapter, and that is the matter of decision making in a household. There are many decisions that must be made regularly, and those decisions can be the source of tremendous tension and disagreement. What's more, couples are making those decisions in the light of much uncertainty concerning the future. "If we buy a house, will the value go up or down? Will our jobs hold steady or provide financial uncertainty?" Those are just two of many examples of the questions that must be faced and whose answers may take a relationship on a roller coaster ride of uncertainty. Against the backdrop of roles and responsibilities, let's look at the practice of decision making to see what we can learn that will help the modern couple navigate these potentially stormy waters.

CHAPTER 8

MAKING DECISIONS

In all relationships, decisions need to be made almost every day. Every decision causes something to happen, something *not* to happen, or something to remain the same. We focus in our sessions on what the modern couple should do when the Bible doesn't specifically address the situation they are facing. For example, it's easy if you are just talking about submission to refer to Ephesians 5. It's also easier when a specific gift or strength is involved like financial planning, gardening, or home décor. What happens, however, when you are talking about what you should do when buying a car, deciding where you're going to live, where you're going to work, or what schools your children will go to (Christian? secular? private? public?)? Those are real and important decisions every family must make.

We have identified 10 questions to help couples make decisions that glorify God and honor one another. Obviously, not every decision will require this kind of attention and scrutiny, but major decisions require significant investments of time and energy. These questions will help guide the process and must be discussed regardless of what decisions couples have already made about roles, responsibilities, submission, and personal strengths.

1. Have you searched for wisdom?

As we start our module on decision making, we urge couples to diligently search out any and all biblical principles exist that could help inform and shape their decisions. That may include introducing them to some basic tools to help them understand where and how to do a Bible search. Also, there are already existing lists of verses that speak to various life issues to which we can refer them.

We begin by looking at Proverbs 2:2-6, which shows them that if they want biblical wisdom for decisions, they will have to pay a price:

> My son, if you accept my words and store up my commands within you, turning your ear to wisdom and applying your heart to understanding—indeed, if you *call out* for insight and *cry aloud* for understanding, and if you *look for it as for silver* and *search for it as for hidden treasure*, then you will understand the fear of the LORD and find the knowledge of God. For the LORD gives wisdom; from his mouth come knowledge and understanding (emphasis added).

The seeking of wisdom we are talking about is not found through a passive, casual approach. Notice the action words in that passage: *call out, cry aloud, look, search.*

It is only when an individual or a couple actively search for wisdom and keep searching until they find it that they will receive it. Now, we are not saying that the Bible addresses all issues, for it won't tell anyone what car to buy or what vacation to take. It will tell us, however, not to go into debt or not to be consumed in our pursuit of material things. One pastor said the Bible is the oldest book whose author is still alive. That Author, the Lord Himself, can impart wisdom through His word for those who want it more than anything else.

Furthermore, God urges couples to seek counsel from people wiser than they are. This is so simple, but so often overlooked. People often think that counseling should be a last resort when things are about to fall apart in their relationship. The book of Proverbs is clear that wisdom should be sought through wise counselors at *all* times: "Walk with the wise and become wise, for a companion of fools suffers harm" (Proverbs 13:20). Therefore, couples should seek marriage counsel, parenting counsel, financial counsel, and professional counsel when times are good and not so good. Don't make mistakes and learn from them; learn from *other* people's mistakes so you won't have to make those mistakes yourself.

When couples reach an impasse, when they have prayed, sought counsel, talked to one another, talked again, and then do all that one more time, there may need to be a mentor couple or voice of wisdom that they can seek. Remember, it's not about winning an argument or one partner getting his or her way, it's about making the best decision possible in the time frame and with the information available.

Many couples fail to spend time planning together. And they should not only plan what they will do if everything goes right, but also if it goes wrong. They should be asking themselves and discussing such things as: Where do we want to be in five years? What are our financial goals? What happens if one of us loses his or her job? What if we are suddenly relocated with a job? What if we have a serious financial setback, like a major repair or loss of an investment? It's called scenario planning, and many plan with the thought that everything is going to stay the same as it is today or get better. While we hope that's the case, very often it is not, and couples are not prepared for what the Bible calls the "day of trouble." Good communication and identification of roles will enhance the ability to handle a crisis.

In the last chapter, we talked about roles, which very often are based on strengths the individuals in the relationship have. We also discussed submission as being the need for both partners to submit to one another according to their gifts. Ultimately, the husband is the authority in the home, and may have to be the one to make certain decisions, like where the family will worship or when the family will have devotions. He never uses his position, however, as a position of power but rather as a opportunity to serve his family members in love.

2. Have you prayed?

There is no such thing as too much prayer. If a couple is seeking wisdom to make a decision, who is better to set the tone and give perspective than the God they are following? Every modern couple should want to place Christ at the center of all their decision making. You want to have Christ and His influence impact everything about which you are thinking. Sometimes you think that something may be important when after you pray and reexamine it, you find it's just not as important as you had thought.

Prayer will also keep a couple from making a premature decision that Proverbs 19:2 warns us about: "Desire without knowledge is not good—how much more will hasty feet miss the way!" We use that verse and others like it to ask our couples if they are making a premature decision. We ask them a related question: Does a decision really have to be made right now?

A lot of times we will make premature decisions out of fear. Don't let the fear of missing out on something drive a decision. Sometimes you may think you have to purchase something today or it might not be there later. In most cases, it will be there or something else will be there, so you don't have to make it today. Beware of once-in-a-lifetime deals, or of needing to have something immediately to satisfy your desire for instant gratification. If you don't know what to do, don't do anything at all. Taking the time to pray will slow down you and the process so you can get a better perspective.

3. What are your values? Are you being true to them?

Being clear about what is important to you goes back to the practice of good communication. If you don't take the time to talk about issues, there are going to be assumptions that come into play, and assumptions are thoughts that don't have a complete or proper perspective. When you assume things, it often leads to misunderstandings. You want to be able to keep the main thing the main thing and work through that first, before you go on to another area.

We give the couples some tips, like avoiding having separate conversations with others, and making sure they are talking about the same thing. For example, both can have a value of "family time," but one thinks that is when the family is on vacation, while the other thinks it is every day. They need to ask questions, get a clear understanding, and acknowledge that each has blind spots. Don't create a hostile atmosphere where one partner is unable to receive what the other is saying.

Family values are those principles that should help guide all decisions. Let's say that a couple has a value of being debt free. Then that value guides all decisions or is at least factored in if debt for a car or home are being considered. If the couple has a value of family first, then that determines where and with whom they will spend their holidays. If they have a value of church participation, then that value may actually determine where they live so they can be closer to a good church.

Often values are assumed but not discussed. We have known families who write out their values and post them for all to see, including the children and visitors to the home. Those values can include statements about eating, exercise, quiet times, family gatherings, work, communication, and any other aspect of family or married life.

We go so far as to say that values are principles that don't require prayer before a decision is made. For example, if the family value is helping the poor, then when an appeal is made due to the needs after a public tragedy or a church family, the value of helping the poor kicks in and one or both of the partners automatically respond.

4. Are you trying to win or find the best outcome?

When you are making decisions, one partner doesn't want to be so locked on to what he or she thinks is best that each one has already figured out what the outcome should be before they go through some discussions. This is the difference between two positions in decision making called inquiry and advocacy. If you are *advocating* for a certain position, that's okay to a certain point. That means you are pushing or reasoning for a specific decision to be made. If one partner is advocating, that can be a good source of all the reasons why something should or should not be done. If that partner's position is set in stone and there is no wiggle room, it can become akin to winning an argument or debate at any cost, no matter what. You can advocate as long as you don't go overboard to lobby and win everyone over to your point of view.

If you're in inquiry mode, you're just looking at the options to find the best way forward. When you are searching and discussing, all the things you learned in the communications chapters must be put to good use. You must ask questions, answer questions, listen, summarize, pray, listen and ask some more, and then take time (when possible) to think more deeply on what was said as it pertains to the decision at hand.

As we mentioned earlier, there are some people who love to debate and win arguments. They are not passionate about the result of the decision, they just want to come out on top. That can lead to a winner-take-all mentality that harms the relationship.

5. Are you listening to one another?
Can you summarize your partner's views?

Once again, you must employ the techniques and disciplines you learned in the previous chapters when you are looking for direction on a decision. Remember our ratio of listening to speaking, which is two to one, based on the fact that you have two ears and one mouth. Listen twice as much as you speak. Ask questions. You may even want to take the position that is the opposite of what you really think, just so you can see if there is anything in the opposing view that will help you see more clearly.

When couples make decisions, it doesn't have to be a zero-sum game. By that, we mean that when one partner gets his or her way, the other one loses, so there is a winner and a loser, adding up to no progress or zero sum. The goal is actually what's referred to as Win/Win, and that's when the decision is a positive for *all* people, thus creating a positive sum as opposed to zero sum.

The goal is a discussion that flows freely without either partner holding on to what he or she said like it is precious metal to be protected at all costs. You place your input into a neutral place, and let it be mixed in with everything else that is said, as opposed to circling the wagons and making it the non-negotiable minimum. There are half of the questions that we give modern couples to ask when a decision is being considered. In the next chapter we will look at the second set of five. We will hold off on our subject review until after we have presented all ten questions.

CHAPTER 9

MORE ON
MAKING DECISIONS

When you think about it, not many decisions are irrevocable. Yes, the decision to have a child is one that is irrevocable (although there are times when we might want to give them away), but where to live, what to drive, in what to invest, where to work, and where a couple will spend the holidays are not irreversible decisions, nor will the effects for good or bad will not last forever. We say that to help them keep decisions in perspective. Yes, they may have to live with some discomfort and pain for a season, but in the Bible it states, "This too shall pass."

Couples can make good decisions not when everything turns out exactly as they anticipated, but when they did all they could to make the best decision. If through no one's fault circumstances change that impact the decision's outcome, it can still be considered a good decision. For example, no one knew when you decided to take a new job that there would be an economic downturn. You made the best decision with the information you had, and God didn't seem to indicate *not* to do it, so that makes it a good decision, even though you have been cut to part-time or let go altogether. Yes, that's painful, but that doesn't mean you made a bad decision.

We say that because we will enter into a discussion of conflict resolution in the next chapter, and sometimes the conflict enters in when there are consequences for decisions that were made. If the consequences "shall pass" with time, then the couple needs to see it all as a faith and love-building exercise—a chance for them to grow as a team and to add their "story" of life together. Having said that, here are the last five questions a couple can use to help them when they are making a decision.

6. Are you encouraging and openly sharing thoughts, feelings, and opinions with love, respect, and kindness?

Remember that you are trying to resolve or solve something. You want to be able to be freely communicating. You don't want to keep rehashing something you haven't fully resolved from the past in anger or bitterness. One partner should say, "If you can show me where your position is stronger, better, and more cost effective, I'm open to revising my view." You are not trying to win a debate or a contest; you are searching for truth as best you see and understand it. Therefore, be civil in your discussions and deliberations.

We show people in our seminars Proverbs 14:1, which states, "The wise woman builds her house, but the foolish tears it down with her own hands." If a partner approaches an issue with a closed mind and goes forth in force, taking no prisoners, then what does that look like once the decision is made? If you get your way, but in the process injure your partner or the relationship, what have you really gained? Encourage one another to freely share thoughts and opinions, and then do so with love, respect, and kindness. Avoid criticism and manipulation of one another. Strive to be open to all expressions without taking offense.

The issue of manipulation is a subtle practice that enters into almost all relationships. If you have an intense discussion with your spouse and then don't speak to him or her for three days, you are trying to gain a concession from your partner using the silent treatment. That's what is called manipulation. Most couples will have disagreements, and one or both may need a cooling off period to get their emotions back in check or to reflect and gain perspective. If that silence lasts more than a day, or if there is constant anger and bickering over the matter, then that may represent one partner's attempt to "strong arm" the other—and women can do that as much as men.

Couples must learn how to talk, argue, discuss, debate, and dialogue with one another, even while they are passionately weighing in on the issues, but not making or taking it personally. If you interject, "You're just like your mother. You're headed just where your father headed," that may be a true statement, but that's another conversation for a different time. Keep the discussion focused on the issue at hand.

7. Are you aware of your attitude and tone?

If you have criticism, disrespect, or anger in your heart, your spouse will hear those things, even when your words are positive. Oftentimes, we will say the right words, but it will be said sarcastically. We have to be aware that when we're in a decision-making mode, we must keep our tone at a level that it doesn't intimidate our partners, or use it to sway or manipulate our partner's decision. You're trying to make a good decision and not win a debate or vanquish your opponent. It's not really important who wins or loses. It's about getting the issue resolved.

Also, the Bible is clear that you are to deal with any anger quickly and ruthlessly, because anger will keep cropping up and ruin the communication you need to make decisions. The Apostle Paul wrote in Ephesians 4:26-27, "In your anger do not sin: Do not let the sun go down while you are still angry, and do not give the devil a foothold." There are times when anger may flare in dialogue. When it does, keep these things in mind:

1. Admit that you are angry.

2. If your partner is angry, don't respond in kind. Acknowledge his or her feelings.

3. Continue to apply the rules of good communication: empathize, listen, repeat, perhaps even saying, "I can see you are angry. I did not

know you felt that strongly about this issue. Tell me more. I will listen and not react."

4. Apply the truth found in Proverbs 15:1: "A gentle answer turns away wrath, but a harsh word stirs up anger."

5. Try to compartmentalize the anger by suggesting "I can see you are angry about this or that. Can we go back to the decision and I promise to revisit this problem that made you angry after that?"

Being aware of what you are feeling and what your partner is feeling will help you make good decisions because you won't be blindsided by hidden issues or discussions that only serve to derail your progress on decisions.

8. Are you listening and requesting clarification when needed?

We discussed this at length in the previous chapters on communication, and we have mentioned it earlier in this decision-making material. A large part of communication is being an active and effective listener. Communication has to have a speaker *and* a listener. We have talked about listening and letting your partner know you are listening. One of the techniques to do that is to repeat back to your partner something he or she said, even if you are paraphrasing it. Listening goes beyond words. It includes body language, posture, tone of voice, and even the place where we should have the discussion.

Speaking of place, you need to find a place where you can turn off your phone and TV, so you will have minimal distractions and will be able to really concentrate on the issues that are in front of you. We don't recommend doing that in a public place, like a restaurant, if the issue is going to be emotionally charged. If you have a quiet place at home, or maybe have someone babysit your children so you can have uninterrupted time to get to the meat of the problems or challenge. Sometimes having an arbiter helps, someone whose opinion both of you value. Sometimes it's a pastor or a mutual friend who you know won't be one-sided, but we would recommend you avoid using family members.

Proverbs 11:14 says, "Where there is no guidance, the people fall, but in abundance of counselors, there is victory, Proverbs 18:1 (NASB) states, "He who separates himself seeks his own desire, he quarrels against all sound wisdom," and Proverbs 18:2 follows up with, "A fool does not delight in understanding, but only in revealing his own mind." Armed with that timeless advice, we urge partners to pay attention to what others say and factor that into their decisions. We don't want them to surrender the independence and uniqueness of their own relationship to others, but we don't want them to float on a sea of ignorance when help is just a holler away.

By now, you are probably thinking, "when will they get off the listening issue?"

The answer is probably not in this book! This is so important not only for the reasons we have mentioned, but it is also an indication of how well the individual partners listen to the Lord! Jesus said,

> "If anyone has ears to hear, let them hear. Consider carefully what you hear," he continued. "With the measure you use, it will be measured to you—and even more. Whoever has will be given more; whoever does not have, even what they have will be taken from them" (Mark 4:23-25).

Jesus was referring to spiritual matters when He said those words, and the source of all spiritual insight is God whether He speaks through His word, through circumstances, or through a still, small voice. We must all cultivate the ability to listen and comprehend first to one another, and then to God, for Paul explained this concept in 1 Corinthians 15:46: "The spiritual did not come first, but the natural, and after that the spiritual." If God is going to get the attention of one of both of the partners to help them with their decisions and in their relationship, they are going to have to learn to listen, first to one another and ultimately to Him!

9. Are you in agreement?

Sometimes a decision has a time limit on it, and one of the partners may need more time. At that point, the one who needs more time may have to make a decision by saying, "I agree that you should make this decision because I am not comfortable, but I can see that you are. I am fine with that." Or that party needs to say, "I need more time, and since we don't have it, I think we need to wait and do nothing." How does anyone know which to say? There are no hard-and-fast rules, and so it goes back to submitting to one another's strengths, and trusting God's guidance that the couple sought.

The point we are making is that couples need to be in general agreement and, if they decide to proceed, not be angry about the results that emerge from the decision. Decision making is an art, not a science. There are many facts and feelings that go into a decision, and partners need to talk it through and arrive at a mutually-agreed upon solution within the time available.

If you can talk it out and one or the other party can persuade the other to see it from a different viewpoint, there is a better chance of being unified. Even when a decision may not be the best, at least it was reached together as a team. It won't be one or the other's fault if the results aren't ideal, because each gave it their best and most thorough consideration.

We talked about being assertive, and we keep mentioning that because often-times there is one party who is more aggressive or assertive than the other. We try to teach the assertive one to actually help the more passive partner speak and contribute, so he or she can sincerely seek and then hear what the other person is thinking. The passive partner doesn't need to say, "Go ahead, I'm fine with whatever decision you make." They may just be afraid of making the wrong decision, and they want the assertive partner to bear the burden if it is wrong. When that builds up, there can be problems. Therefore, the meek or quiet partner must learn to weigh in on the issue, and the assertive partner can help that happen.

A lot of decision making will be based on how well the partners know each other. If you know that one partner's decision making in a particular area has turned out well in the past, and you know that's how he or she operates, then the decision making shouldn't be that difficult. You can rely on them in that scenario.

10. Are you open to a course adjustment?

We are repeating ourselves here, but we cannot emphasize enough how counterproductive it is to relationships and good decision making when one partner enters into a discussion with his or her mind made up. It is important, once the decision is made, to review it at some point to see if a better decision can be made the next time. You will be able to learn from your mistakes because as a couple, mistakes are going to be made and misunderstandings are going to happen. When you review and debrief, it should not only be the decision itself, but *how* the decision was reached. Could we have taken more time? Did one partner push the decision through, and the results were not the best? Were we patient enough to get all the information we needed? In hindsight, were there other people we could have consulted? Of those we did consult, who had the best advice so we can seek them out again later?

For example, we sat down and looked at the decision we made to live in our current house. The decision was made to purchase it, but we said we would live there for only a short period of time, something like five years. We knew it was a starter house, and we wanted to get our boys through high school and into college. Then we were moving on because that's not where we wanted to be. Twenty-some years later we're still there.

Now we look back and realize that our family background impacted our thinking. I [Helen] grew up in housing projects, while my husband did not. I [Helen] didn't want to go back to the projects. Jack had no way of knowing that was my [Helen's] thought process. Jack would jump out in the deep and have faith. Looking back, the decision to move on quickly was the right strategy, but I [Helen] had a lot of fear. Now we're twenty-something years down the road and have not moved because of that fear. We are not arguing over that and we have discussed it openly and honestly. Right now, our finances preclude a move, but one day, we are "movin' on up to the East Side!"

Another thing that can help when you have to make a decision is to have a contingency plan. If you have to make adjustments or if something falls through the cracks unexpectedly, you have at least given some thought to a plan to have something to fall back on. Often we make decisions without assessing the risks, and it can end up being a poor decision (or a good decision with an unforeseen negative outcome). We're also big advocates for assessing the risk and having a contingency plan in case the bottom falls out and the downside of the risk comes true.

As we stated at the start of this chapter, most decisions are not terminal or fatal. Since couples are in a long-term relationship, they will have together plenty of time, Lord willing, so they can learn from it. We as a couple are still learning one another's tendencies and recognizing our strengths and weaknesses where decision making is concerned. We now realize that Jack needs a lot of time to make decisions. If we need to get the kids in a better school a year from now, we better start discussing that now. Neither one of us can be the only one to make a mistake, where my mistakes are excusable but his are not! We are going to learn and grow, and we must go back to evaluate how the decision was made. If the negative outcome was unavoidable, we live with it. If it was avoidable, we learn from it.

For your review and reference, here are the 10 questions couples should ask as they approach any decisions they face:

1. Have you searched for wisdom?

2. Have you prayed?

3. What are your values? Are you being true to them?

4. Are you trying to win or find the best outcome?

5. Are you listening to one another? Can you summarize your partner's views?

6. Are you encouraging and openly sharing thoughts, feelings, and opinions with love, respect, and kindness?

7. Are you aware of your attitude and tone?

8. Are you listening and requesting clarification when needed?

9. Are you in agreement?

10. Are you open to a course adjustment?

We are confident that these questions will help you make good decisions, but the process is not perfect or foolproof. Because that's true, we will address an important issue in the next section, and that is the importance of knowing how to resolve a conflict when it arises.

CHAPTER 10

CONFLICT RESOLUTION

We attempt to establish something we call the ladder effect in our seminars. We want each session to build off the previous one, so our participants feel like they are growing and making progress, which they are. You can tell that we have established communication as the lower ladder rungs, and now we are getting up to the higher rungs that require more skill. The higher anyone goes on a ladder, the more risk there is, but the closer the climber reaches his or her objective. Conflict resolution is near the top, because if couples don't learn how to handle the inevitable disagreements that can escalate into major conflict, their relationship is in great danger.

No matter how well partners communicate, define roles and make decisions, there are bound to be conflicts that arise, some more serious than others. Our goal is to help the couples discuss whatever issues they are having and to trust God that a resolution will emerge if they don't panic or dig their heels in to insist that what happens *must* be what one or the other wants.

One of the bigger misconceptions a modern couple can have is that they don't think a good relationship has any conflict in it. We try to modify that assumption right away. In *any* kind of relationship, there will be some type of misunderstandings and some issues of what direction to go. The other misconception people have is that conflict is automatically negative. That is also not necessarily true.

The problem with conflict is that a lot of emotion gets involved in conflict, especially when people are comfortable with one another. That's why family squabbles can be the worst kind of disputes. People have high expectations of how they will be treated, and those expectations can be idealistic when it comes to family and marriage. Everyone believes they are going to live happily ever after, and when that doesn't happen, they sometimes assume it is the other person's fault. They believe they made a mistake and married the wrong person. It goes back to what we said earlier. Marriage takes place between two foreigners, who come together out of their personal family cultures to synthesize a new family unit and culture. That is tough work and conflicts will arise along the way. That doesn't mean there is something wrong; it simply indicates that the couples are establishing something new, for which there is no exact roadmap to follow.

Sometimes conflict causes couples to reassess where they are and then set some new ground rules so they can move on and continue to grow and mature. The most important thing we try to do in our sessions is to help them establish new techniques that will help them have discussions that are less emotionally-charged. Once again, we go back to work on listening skills, so they can hopefully clearly understand and diffuse the problem, and then come to some type of positive resolution.

At the same time, we want them to understand that conflict does not have to be the norm. It happens, but we don't want them getting addicted to the drama, the emotional rush that comes from a battle of wills. Some grew up in home relationships that were full of conflict, so some people actually believe that is how marriage is supposed to be. Conflict is inevitable but it doesn't have to be endless and repetitive. What's more, it can be a learning and growth experience that strengthens a relationship and prepares the couple for when the next crisis or conflict may appear.

We pay special attention to helping couples understand anger, and use it as their ally and not as a bludgeon or weapon, as we discussed in the previous chapter. Many people grew up around anger and felt the effects of it. They saw someone batter someone else (verbally or literally) because of anger, or they saw anger come out when someone had been drinking. Therefore, people associate anger with bad things because they only saw bad things happen in an angry environment. We want men and women to see that good things can come from anger, *if* the angry person uses the anger as a motivation to improve or do better or seek and find a resolution.

If you look at the scale and see you gained 10 pounds, that can make you angry. The wrong reaction to that fact is to throw the scale against the wall. The better expression of anger would be to finally do something about losing weight. The bad anger over missing out on a promotion is to hold a grudge or to seek revenge. The good affect would be to finally return to school so that you are not passed over again. In a relationship, anger can drive you to talk about the problem and resolve to find a solution—or it can be like throwing gasoline on a fire.

Sometimes the anger has deep roots and it doesn't take much for that anger to come to the surface whenever certain stimuli are present in a relationship. One of the things I [Jack] like to have couples talk about is what makes each one angry. Many times those issues might seem unimportant to the other partner. To the angered partner, however, they are very important, so we try to help them discover what their anger triggers are. If they can learn to look at themselves, as opposed to looking at their partner in times of anger, it tends to give a different view of what is causing the anger. Our goal is to get each partner to ask, "Do I have a role in the situation and in these things that are making me angry?" At times, they do not, but it's a good place to start by starting with any personal responsibility.

And of course, sometimes the one spouse is not really angry at his or her partner. That's not their problem. They have unresolved issues with another person, usually a parent, previous partner, teacher, or some other person who was an authority figure in their life. When the one partner says, "Hurry up!", the other partner may get angry. They may not realize any longer that they are still angry because their mother always hurried them, or berated or spanked them for being late, so when their spouse enters into that particular scenario, they are on the receiving end of a reaction that is caused by some unresolved issue from the past. We try to help couples isolate those instances. Sometimes, additional counseling is necessary to identify and isolate root causes, but our goal is to at least allow the partners to start the process by asking, "What makes me angry and why? What or who am I really angry about here?"

As stated earlier, anger in and of itself is not wrong or sinful. Anger is a human emotion that God gave to motivate us. The problem comes in when it motivates us to do the wrong thing. If it is to throw the vase against the wall, then we have misused the anger. If it forces us to sit down and talk with someone or to go to the gym, or get some help, then the anger in and of itself is positive. Too often people misinterpret the anger, and feel like when they are angry, they have sinned or fallen short. Some couples falsely believe that they should never be angry with one another, but we have found that to be unrealistic.

With some people, anger is the only time when they are motivated to speak. They may be cool, calm, and collected for ten years, and suddenly they go off when a certain straw breaks the camel's back, so to speak. Then their partner isn't ready for that strong of a reaction and the argument begins. Sometimes people have trouble processing their emotions and don't know when or how to say something that may lead to conflict. So they wait until they are really angry, erupt, and then have a mess to clean up. Then they speak in absolute terms, and say things like, "You always," or "You never," or "I have asked you a million times not to do that." Or one airs past grievances that should have been dealt with by keeping short accounts, but because the anger gives them permission and somehow validates what they are sharing, the opportunity for real communication is lost. Then the accused tries to dispute those statements and the conflict intensifies with both trying to "win the argument."

When we talk about the straw that broke the camel's back, we point out that if one straw broke your camel's back, something was already accumulating so that you had way too many straws before that. Or we try to help them see that they need a stronger camel, because if the slightest thing is going to set them off, it's a deeper problem. Anger is not sinful, but what we do with it is very often is inappropriate and may even lead to sinful behavior.

If we can help the angry partner take responsibility for his or her anger, then there is a chance for the partners to engage in dialogue. Misunderstandings occur when people aren't communicating properly. That brings us back to chapters three through six, when we work on establishing healthy communication.

If one partner's problem is his or her mother or father, then taking it out on the partner isn't going to solve the issue. They have to get the root of the problem. We are not trying to teach techniques or allow a marriage to be dependent on people outside the household, but we want the couple to recognize when they may need outside help. Sometimes they need an individual session with someone to objectively, in the presence of God, look at all the issues of why they are spending so much money, why another *won't* spend money, why he *won't* discipline the children, why she won't *stop* disciplining the children. Very often there are some other root causes.

Modern couples shouldn't be surprised that they have issues that lead to conflict. We all do. Sometimes those issues are not revealed until the circumstances come up. When we first get together, we have so much in common. Then the first child comes, and no couple knows how they are going to respond to the problems that first child will have until they encounter them. That's going to uncover issues. Then the one partner says, "you've changed," and that may be true. But that tendency to respond may have been there all along but had no opportunity to come out. The circumstances weren't there for them to face the reality of what was there all along.

Another time the family has a financial crisis and one of the partners doesn't respond very well. Then one says, "He is a monster" or "she is out of control." That's why we have to make a commitment to one another in the covenant of marriage *before* there is conflict, and many people today don't understand that.

Let's review what we talked about in this chapter before we move on to continue our discussion on conflict resolution in the next chapter:

1. Conflict is not necessarily bad or negative if it is handled properly and leads to growth.

2. Anger is not necessarily bad or negative, as long as it is a motivator to find help or answers.

3. Real-life circumstances that have never been previously encountered can reveal what is in a person's heart that was there all along, but never had the opportunity to express.

4. We must examine the root causes of some conflict, which may not be the present relationship, but something from the past that is unresolved.

CHAPTER 11

MORE ON CONFLICT RESOLUTION

We have many modern couples in our seminars who have lived with one another without taking the step to formalize their relationship through marriage vows. We tell those people that we don't care if they have lived together for 20 years. Until they make the commitment and close the door of escape by saying they will never leave, they will *never* truly see their real partner. There is some aspect of their personality that they aren't going to show because they don't want their partner to leave, or they haven't revealed it because the circumstances aren't right. This reality plays tricks on couples all the time.

They think or say, "Oh, we've lived together eight years because I want to know how he trims his toenails. I want to know how she responds sexually." They may find those things, but they still don't really know that person. They won't know them fully, until their child is so sick that she can't pay attention to his sexual needs. They won't know until his family gets into financial problems and he sneaks money to them to help out without her knowledge. They won't know how their partner will respond until the circumstances are present to reveal that.

Let's look at 1 Corinthians 13, perhaps the most famous words about love in the world (that's no exaggeration). Here is what Paul wrote in verses 4 through 8:

> Love is patient, love is kind. It does not envy, it does not boast, it is not proud. It does not dishonor others, it is not self-seeking, it is not easily angered, it keeps no record of wrongs. Love does not delight in evil but rejoices with the truth. It always protects, always trusts, always hopes, always perseveres. Love never fails.

We have not really mentioned love up to this point, but most people are familiar with romantic love. We have songs about it, make movies about it, and some spend their whole life looking for it. When they think they have found it, they talk about finding their soul mate, their "true love." Then that true love goes bankrupt, forgets a special occasion, or seems to be more committed to his bowling league or her exercise class than the romantic relationship. When that happens, they think, "We aren't in love any longer. We need to split up because we have irreconcilable differences."

The problem is that the couple never made the transition from romantic love to what is talked about in 1 Corinthians 13, which is agape (pronounced ah-GAH-pay). It's a Greek word that indicates a deeper, more self-sacrificing love. This is a love that is not characterized by what someone can get but what he or she can give. Look at the words and phrases used in 1 Corinthians 13, ones like "patient," "kind," "no envy," "no boasting," "no pride," "no dishonor," "no self-seeking," "not easily angered," and "no record of wrongs." Agape love always protects, trusts, hopes, perseveres, and never fails. That is the kind of love that solves conflict, not in the spirit of self-interest, but in the interests of others.

We are not advocating that anyone stay in an abusive relationship, or one where there is illegal or immoral activity going on that one partner refuses to stop. Where there is inevitable relational conflict, however, neither party is free to leave simply because things get tough. That's when both people learn about agape love, and get past the romantic love that is so glorified in our culture, but so fickle in the day of trouble that each modern couple will certainly face

Agape love is one party saying, "I'm not part of the problem, but now I am part of the solution. I didn't hurt you like your father did, but I will be part of your healing because I agape love you," or "I didn't hurt you, your mother hurt you. You should not take it out on me. But I'm not here to be a part of the problem. My agape love commitment to you is that we're going to walk through this together."

A great time to lay this foundation for agape love is during premarital counseling, which many couples, especially live-in couples, did not usually have. They enter into the relationship and figure it will all work out. During premarital counseling, we can find out what other relationships there have been in an individual's past that may impact their new relationship. There may be past hurt, anger, fear, or resentment from a previous lover, spouse, or parent. All that needs to be addressed before they enter into marriage, and sometimes it requires special counseling to do so. Doing that can prevent a lot of conflict later when the proper foundation is laid.

Couples that learn how to resolve conflict must learn to accept that each one is part of the problem, or at least be willing to see that. There are cases where it is all the other person's fault, but there aren't many. Jesus gave us the principle to follow in this when He said,

> "Do not judge, or you too will be judged. For in the same way you judge others, you will be judged, and with the measure you use, it will be measured to you. Why do you look at the speck of sawdust in your brother's eye and pay no attention to the plank in your own eye? How can you say to your brother, 'Let me take the speck out of your eye,' when all the time there is a plank in your own eye? You hypocrite, first take the plank out of your own eye, and then you will see clearly to remove the speck from your brother's eye" (Matthew 7:1-5).

The Bible tells us that we should take the plank out of our own eye before we try to do eye surgery on someone else. It's easy to point out what the other party is doing wrong. The harder part is learning why you're in conflict and accepting your role in the conflict. What did you have to do with it? You can get outside help and mediators, but ultimately, the couple has to decide that each one cannot allow children, in-laws, jobs, or church responsibilities to come between them. *You* are the one who has to resolve the problem. Partners have to genuinely apologize and move on, and they have to genuinely forgive. Part of that moving on is leaving it in the past. If the situation arises again, neither partner will dredge that up as a point of contention in the conflict. You have to learn how to approach each problem on its own terms, and not keep bringing up past displeasures and add them to the current issue.

We have also found an interesting dynamic with couples who are upwardly mobile, or highly skilled or anointed for ministry. They often use the area of conflict as a competition to see who will win and who will come out ahead. They never really address the issue, because the competitive urge overtakes them. We help them realize when that may be happening, and a tool we use is to help in that area is something called the *Thomas Kilman Conflict Profile*. We also use the DISC personality assessment to help people understand their personalities and their tendencies of how they may respond when conflict is present. Some wade into conflict and enjoy it; others avoid it at all costs. Some respond out of their fear of rejection and others from their fear of being wrong or incorrect. Knowing that will help any couple when it comes to conflict.

We have found some couples have one party who is addicted to the drama of conflict. That is all they ever observed, or how they learned to relate to others. We help them get to the root of what's causing that, or they will always bring their relationship back to the point of tension. We ask them to consider the questions, "Why can't you allow yourself to be happy? Why? You can't allow yourself to be satisfied. Why?" Everything will be going along smoothly, and then out of the blue they bring themselves back to the place of problems or conflict. Formerly, we conducted some breakouts where Helen would talk to the women and give them time to really open up. When they did, some serious things came out about their relationships with their fathers or with other men in their lives. She discovered some of the women would trust a man up to a certain point but no more, and that has caused a lot of conflict.

Another exercise we use with them is called "The 10 Step Worksheet for Resolving Conflict." Each partner fills it out and then we bring them back together so they can compare their answers. It presents them with some questions, like "What were some of your past attempts to solve an issue that were not successful?", or "How did you contribute to a certain problem or conflict?" We're not asking them to blame each other, but to own up or acknowledge their part in it. We also ask them to choose one particular issue that they would like to see resolved. We found that in some cases, the partners weren't even aware that it was an issue because there was no communication about it.

Another thing we do is give them homework to establish a set meeting time when they won't be interrupted so they can sit down and go over issues. It's important that a specific time is set so both can be prepared and neither person feels like he or she has been blind-sided by one party pressing for a response or an intense talk. They may even build an agenda throughout the week for their set meeting. If they can't get agreement and feel the problem wasn't resolved, they can set another day and go over that problem again—or carry it over to the next week's meeting.

We also encourage using humor. We like to say, "If it's going to funny later, then it's funny now. Laugh!" We had one couple who were super serious, and that was part of their problem. We asked them to look back to when they were dating and things were more laid back and fun. We asked them to consider how they could recapture that dynamic now? They worked on that, and we found again that a date night can be very helpful.

We encourage men and women to pay attention to see if they notice their partner working on what caused the conflict. If they see their partner making positive steps towards resolving it, we urge them to praise their efforts. We also remind them to keep their conflict and things that go on in their marriage to themselves. They should not call their mother or sister or girlfriends or guy friends to gossip about their partner. The problem then is that when the couple resolves the conflict, the family or friends remember what a no-good rascal the one partner is according to the other partner's gossip report. Marriage is not a spectator sport, and others should not be invited to view the conflict and choose sides. Partners should look for allies of their relationship, not personal allies for one partner for or against the other.

What did we learn in this chapter? We learned:

1. The goal of any couple's relationship is agape love and not only romantic love.

2. Both partners must approach a problem or conflict with an openness to what he or she may be contributing to the problem.

3. It is helpful for each partner to understand his or her personality and how he or she has been conditioned to respond to conflict, which may be to wade into it or avoid it at all costs.

4. Couples must work at having fun together!

Perhaps you have read up to this point and thought to yourself (or out loud), "I wonder when they will talk about sex?" The good news is that the answer is "In the next chapter!" Let's go there now.

SECTION FIVE

SEX, KIDS,
AND MONEY

CHAPTER 12

INTIMACY

During this session entitled *Intimacy*, we want the modern couple to understand the power in intimacy and the privilege and responsibilities involved in developing that kind of relationship. We also want them to learn about the differences between women and men (beyond the obvious physical difference) and see how those differences can be drawn on to strengthen their relationship. Our goal, as always, is to help them learn techniques to enhance their time together. We already began our discussion in the section on communication, but let's continue it now, since it is the unique action that characterizes married couples.

We found in a lot of Christian homes and relationships that sex is viewed as taboo or "dirty." By this point in our seminar, we have already showed that the Bible addresses sex and intimacy in many places. Apparently, sex must be not only acceptable but holy if the Bible endorses it and gives instructions where sex is concerned. We also utilize a worksheet that allows couples to examine some of their ideas about intimacy and discover how they developed those attitudes, whether it was through their parents, home, or school.

Some men and women are surprised to learn that intimacy encompasses more than just sex. Certainly sex is a part of it, but from a biblical standpoint, intimacy was intended not only for procreation, but also for pleasure and even for protection. Men and women differ in their expectations of and approach to sexual intimacy, and we want to explore those differences so they can add to and not detract from both partners growing closer together to fulfill the biblical mandate that "two shall become one flesh." That's important because marital intimacy is a gift from God.

Let's look again at Ephesians 5, but this time examine the entire passage that speaks to marriage to see what it has to say about intimacy:

Wives, submit yourselves to your own husbands as you do to the Lord. For the husband is the head of the wife as Christ is the head of the church, his body, of which he is the Savior. Now as the church submits to Christ, so also wives should submit to their husbands in everything.

Husbands, love your wives, just as Christ loved the church and gave himself up for her to make her holy, cleansing her by the washing with water through the word, and to present her to himself as a radiant church, without stain or wrinkle or any other blemish, but holy and blameless. In this same way, husbands ought to love their wives as their own bodies. He who loves his wife loves himself.

After all, no one ever hated their own body, but they feed and care for their body, just as Christ does the church—for we are members of his body. "For this reason a man will leave his father and mother and be united to his wife, and the two will become one flesh." This is a profound mystery—but I am talking about Christ and the church. However, each one of you also must love his wife as he loves himself, and the wife must respect her husband (Ephesians 5:22-33).

The intimacy between a husband and wife is a model of the love between Christ and His church. That is why there is to be sexual purity and loyalty, if we can use that word, between a husband and wife, and among all God's people, whether married or single. There can be nothing that supplants or supersedes anyone's relationship with Christ. It is the highest priority. The marriage relationship mirrors that singleness of commitment, and is to be a source of instruction and reflection for anyone who desires to understand more about the relationship between Christ and His bride, also known as the Church. Nothing on earth can reflect that kind of relationship except for the one between a husband and wife.

Paul gave some sexual instructions for husbands and wives, which sometimes surprises the couples with whom we work. They often don't believe the Bible has *anything* to say about sex, but it does. Here is one of the things that Paul wrote:

> But since sexual immorality is occurring, each man should have sexual relations with his own wife, and each woman with her own husband. The husband should fulfill his marital duty to his wife, and likewise the wife to her husband. The wife does not have authority over her own body but yields it to her husband. In the same way, the husband does not have authority over his own body but yields it to his wife. Do not deprive each other except perhaps by mutual consent and for a time, so that you may devote yourselves to prayer. Then come together again so that Satan will not tempt you because of your lack of self-control (1 Corinthians 7:2-5).

Notice what Paul said about sex:

- It should occur within the boundaries of marriage.

- It is the *duty* of both the husband and the wife to have sex with each other.

- Neither the husband nor the wife has absolute control over his or her body; both partners should have a voice in the act of sex.

- Neither partner has the right to deprive the other of sex.

- Satan is active and will try to ruin God's righteous act between the husband and wife.

- The sex drive is almost uncontrollable without God's help and the help of each marriage partner.

You may see more than those six points in 1 Corinthians 7, but you can see that Paul in the Bible had a lot of insight into God's purpose for sex and intimacy.

We mentioned earlier that marital sex is for protection because God created man and woman to be sexual beings, but only within the confines of marriage. To ignore that fact is to ignore God's will, and open one's self up for serious problems. The husband and wife have a duty to protect one another from inappropriate physical relationships outside of their own: "Now to the unmarried and the widows I say: It is good for them to stay unmarried, as I do. But if they cannot control themselves, they should marry, for it is better to marry than to burn with passion" (1 Corinthians 7:8-9).

The concept of "burning with passion" means that if the sex drive is not channeled into marriage, it will find other ways to express itself, and that will lead to all kinds of problems. When you think of it, there would be no sexual communicable diseases if one man and one woman were faithful to each other sexually within the bond of marriage. (The Bible also recognizes that God gives grace to those who are celibate—called to be single—so that they may control their sexual urges.)

When we start to talk about sex, it's awkward initially. Many times, we use videos from TV comedy sitcoms that show some of the humor in each partner's role in or view of intimacy, and that loosen the couples up a bit. We have found that women are generally more open to talk about intimacy than are men. Once again, we always refer back to communication and other skills we have taught them in previous sessions. By this point in our seminar, the couples have usually developed more trust, so they aren't so guarded.

While the women are open to talk, it's difficult for them to talk in front of their husbands for two reasons. One is that they do not want to hurt his feelings or make him feel bad in any way. The other is that it can be difficult to face and admit the fact that there have been some intimacy issues, especially if they have been married for a long time. We had one couple in our sessions who had been married for many decades. According to the wife, she thought things sexually were only so-so, while the husband thought things were great. The wife was thinking, "Well, it's too late to tell him at this point." She was open to tell us, but hesitant to tell him. We worked with them so they could sit down across the table from each other and address that openly and honestly.

It helps if one or the other partner actually inquires about how he or she is doing sexually. That makes it easier for the other partner to speak honestly and without fear. "How are we doing physically? Am I meeting your needs? Is there anything you need to tell me?" Then if the partner can listen without interrupting, defending, or getting his or her feelings hurt, there can be the kind of communication that causes both to grow. That kind of communication is actually part of intimacy. It is being naked before one another not just without clothes but without excuses or half-truths.

In the movie *City Slickers*, Billy Crystal had this to say about sex, "A man just needs a place, a woman needs a reason." The man needs to understand that what motivates or drives him sexually is not the same for his woman and vice versa. We read one marriage counselor who said to the man, "Whatever you want to do while having sex, whatever comes 'naturally,' is probably *not* what your wife wants!" To learn what she does want requires communication; for that kind of information to be communicated requires intimacy and actually leads to more intimacy. The husband must respect the wife's wishes, and the wife must do the same. Part of that respect is found when both partners are considerate of each other's needs.

We heard someone say once that a man wants to see his wife *physically* naked while a woman wants to see her husband *emotionally* naked and able to share. We have found that to be usually true, and it points out the major difference that God built into men and women. Men are all about the physical act. Women have an emotional need in the relationship for intimacy to occur. He is turned on visually, but she is stimulated through intimate discussion and sharing of feelings. She has to be careful not to mother him when he's sharing his thoughts, and he has to be careful not to want her to perform for him sexually regardless of what she is feeling or going through.

If both are considerate of the other person and what his or her needs are and what he or she is feeling, if both want to bring joy and happiness to their partner, then both should be communicating and working hard to find out how each one can please the other. Maybe one partner likes to hold hands in public. Maybe one partner likes to go out, while the other likes to stay in. One likes to cuddle and kiss, the other likes to plan for intimacy well in advance so they can decorate the bedroom or spend the night away from home in a hotel.

Most men consider intimacy just to be sexual. They didn't look at intimacy being a total package. There was a book published years ago with the title, *Sex Begins in the Kitchen*. The author was telling men that if they waited until they got to the bedroom to woo their wives, they were going to be disappointed. They had to start by complimenting her first thing in the morning, by helping to get the kids off to school or by filling or emptying the dishwasher. For the wife, it begins by greeting the husband and talking about his day. It continues by sending a text message to him during the day, telling him that she loves him and is praying for him. Intimacy is more than sex; sex is an expression of intimacy, but not the only expression.

The biblical equivalent of intimacy is the old-fashioned word *knowing*. It says in older translations of the Bible that a man "knew" his wife when they had intimate relations. If you go all the way to the core root of intimacy, it's about knowing. It's knowing the other person as best you can at that point in your relationship, knowing who they are, what they like, what they prefer. We try to get the men to see and to learn some of the things they can do to become closer to their partner. We encourage men to plan surprises, where they can get away from the daily routine with their partner. We equip men to hold better conversations, because part of intimacy is having a feeling of security, where both know how the other feels about each other, and that he or she is the only one.

We work with some young modern couples who have small children, and those kids can be intimacy killers. If you have children, you know that to be true. We're not just talking about them running into the room while the husband and wife are having sex. We're talking about times when the kids are sick or the time involved in getting them to school on time and with all assignments completed. We walk them through what they can expect after they bring the baby home and what that looks like (in other words, when they can have sex again). A woman needs to know that a man can feel rejected when a baby comes into the house, and the man needs to know that a woman is not going to desire intimacy unless she knows the children are cared for adequately. We address learning how to manage expectations where intimacy in concerned.

Because divorce is common and premarital sex is rampant, we find it necessary to address the issue of previous sexual relationships. We encourage partners to talk about previous relationships, if they do so voluntarily. We don't necessarily search or probe for that information, but it's something that needs to be addressed. We have found it's much easier to address those issues when the couples are apart. As facilitators, we also have to let them know that confidentiality is our vow and seal of secrecy. There may be times when a couple can get back together and talk about something that needs to be revealed, or seek some healing that needs to occur from the past. The men are usually a little more reticent to talk. They may have been hurt by a past relationship, but they are hesitant to talk about it because they are supposed to be tough. If they are bringing their old relationship into the new one, however, that needs to be discussed.

Then there is the issue of molestation or past sexual traumas that may be hindering intimacy between a husband and wife. In one seminar, it emerged that the wife had been molested by a family member as a young child. The husband was not aware of this situation, and the woman thought because she was mature that it was a non-issue and there were no ramifications. To the contrary, she began to see that it was a roadblock to her intimately surrendering to her husband.

After counseling and pastoral care, she and her husband are doing quite well. They're growing, but they had to walk through some issues together. That's an expression of intimacy, but the lack of transparent communication was costing them something in the bedroom, and it was taking a toll on their relationship. Sometimes people who have traumatic issues from their past have a lot of sexual guilt. Those things have to be identified and discussed, so the partners can mature in their relationship.

We know premarital sex is the norm of the day, but it's not a biblical norm. No couple can justify living together by using the Bible. To live together, they have to ignore what the Bible says. If they are cohabiting, we are of the opinion that they need move toward marriage because God doesn't endorse sexual relationships between non-married individuals. We don't have our heads buried in the sand and know that premarital sex is a common occurrence, and we don't condemn or judge anyone. If you remember, we had to face this issue when we started dating, and we had been single after our divorces for quite a while. Sex was tempting, but we waited, and we are glad we did!

Sexual relationships outside of marriage is what's referred to as fornication. What's more, cohabiting isn't a preventative for divorce once a man and woman get married. We hear all the time that couples living together can get to know each other, but that plan hasn't worked. We saw a survey in a national newspaper that stated a great percentage of people who live together before marriage actually had greater problems later in their marriage than those who did not.

Also, extramarital affairs are not healthy for any marriage, and what's more, pornography is a problem as well. The Bible is clear about sex outside of marriage: "Marriage should be honored by all, and the marriage bed kept pure, for God will judge the adulterer and all the sexually immoral" (Hebrews 13:4).

We have encountered more than a few modern couples who have experienced an extramarital affair and we try to help them see what caused it. Sometimes it was a lack of maturity. The husband was not mature and ready to be fully committed to the marriage. It didn't have anything to do with love. Another husband said that he really loved his wife, but his wife responded that she couldn't understand why he cheated on her if he loved her. She could not understand how he could separate love and sex, because for her, it was impossible. For him, it was not.

It's rare in the encounters with those who experienced affairs when the woman cheated on the man. In almost every case, it was the husband and he usually expresses great sorrow. It wasn't about a lack of love or caring for his partner. In almost every case, the man felt he was missing something that the wife wasn't giving them—and it wasn't sex. Now that's always an easy excuse for the man to use, and we send couples, and sometimes only the man, for counseling to try and sort out his heart issues. That's also why we spend so much time early in our seminar getting them to communicate with one another, and how not to go outside their relationship to seek answers in the midst of a dispute.

Modern couples also must understand that they will both change as they grow older. Women are going to go through menopause and the man is going to face a mid-life crisis. He will have to face the fact that he's getting older, and that has an impact on his psyche. Both partners will change sexually as well, and often the wife doesn't have the desire to be intimate as she once had—and that can happen to the husband as well. It's not going to all stay the same, and their needs aren't going to stay the same. When changes start coming, they may not recognize them since they're subtle. They don't wake up one day with a mid-life crisis or menopausal stage. That's where they start looking to get back in touch with youth which is long gone.

What did we learn in this chapter? Here are a few review points:

1. Sex is not only acceptable but holy. The Bible endorses it and provides a lot instruction where sex is concerned.

2. A man wants to see his wife *physically* naked while a woman wants to see her husband *emotionally* naked and able to share.

3. Premarital and extra-marital sex are the norms of the day, but they are not the biblical norms.

The Bible does have a lot to say about intimacy, so before we move on to a discussion of children, let's take a closer, deeper look at those Bible references to sex.

CHAPTER 13

MORE BIBLE

We are careful not to become marriage counselors beyond what is appropriate, and try to refer couples to professionals who can help them beyond what we can do. We can pray, facilitate, and encourage those that they are not alone in their struggles, that every couple faces challenges, often greater challenges than they anticipated. When that becomes apparent, they need friends, and they need counselors who can help them navigate the rough waters. We are both pastors, however, so we know there is power and help in the word of God, so we do spend some time looking at more places where the Bible addresses the issues of intimacy and sex. Here are some of the passages that we refer to, which you may want to use to do more study on your own.

1. **Genesis 1:27-28:** So God created mankind in his own image, in the image of God he created them; male and female he created them. God blessed them and said to them, "Be fruitful and increase in number; fill the earth and subdue it. Rule over the fish in the sea and the birds in the sky and over every living creature that moves on the ground."

God created human beings as male and female, and that is the source of historic marriage between one man and one woman. Notice that God gave the man and woman work to do together, so that they would learn to work with one another, and grow in intimacy as they beheld the work of their hands.

2. **Genesis 2:18:** The LORD God said, "It is not good for the man to be alone. I will make a helper suitable for him."

This is where we get the truth that God instituted marriage and sex. He created the woman to be with a man, and once again directed them to focus on their work together of building a relationship, contributing to the world around them, and raising their children.

3. **Genesis 2:24-25:** "That is why a man leaves his father and mother and is united to his wife, and they become one flesh. Adam and his wife were both naked, and they felt no shame."

It is interesting to us how much shame is involved in marriage relationships when the original couple were totally exposed and vulnerable to one another and felt no shame. It is clear that shame entered into their relationship after Adam and Eve sinned. Therefore, we see that God wants men and women to get back to their original state of openness with one another, emotionally and physically. We also see in that passage that there is a unity, described as "one flesh," between a husband and wife. That is an obvious reference to sex, but is not limited to that expression of oneness between a husband and wife.

4. **Genesis 3:16-19:** "To the woman he [God] said, 'I will make your pains in childbearing very severe; with painful labor you will give birth to children. Your desire will be for your husband, and he will rule over you.' To Adam he said, 'Because you listened to your wife and ate fruit from the tree about which I commanded you, 'You must not eat from it,' 'Cursed is the ground because of you; through painful toil you will eat food from it all the days of your life. It will produce thorns and thistles for you, and you will eat the plants of the field. By the sweat of your brow you will eat your food, until you return to the ground, since from it you were taken; for dust you are and to dust you will return."

There were consequences to Adam and Eve's fall that are still being felt in the context of family relationships to this day. From this passage, we see them listed: 1) pain in childbirth; 2) male tendency to dominate, woman's tendency to enable; 3) Adam's proclivity for his identity to be through his work; 4) work is promised to be difficult, not yielding what man desires; 5) man's desire to provide for his own needs as opposed to trusting God for those needs; and 6) death. Many people question whether the Genesis account is a fable, but we see it as the only rational explanation for the condition of the world today, including those in the modern couple and family.

5. **Matthew 19:5:** *"For this reason a man will leave his father and mother and be united to his wife, and the two will become one flesh."*

We include this because it is an example of Jesus referring to this truth found in Genesis 2:24-25. If Jesus referred to it, He must have believed it to be true and still relevant today!

6. **Proverbs 5:15-20:** Drink water from your own cistern, running water from your own well. Should your springs overflow in the streets, your streams of water in the public squares? Let them be yours alone, never to be shared with strangers. May your fountain be blessed, and may you rejoice in the wife of your youth. A loving doe, a graceful deer— may her breasts satisfy you always, may you ever be intoxicated with her love. Why, my son, be intoxicated with another man's wife? Why embrace the bosom of a wayward woman?

The wisdom writer in Proverbs makes a blatant reference to a husband and wife's sexual relationship when he urged men to be satisfied with his wife, being careful not to look to others to provide for him what God intended his wife to provide. This also indicates that the wife is not to withhold her affections from her husband.

7. **Song of Solomon 4:1-7:** How beautiful you are, my darling! Oh, how beautiful! Your eyes behind your veil are doves. Your hair is like a flock of goats descending from the hills of Gilead. Your teeth are like a flock of sheep just shorn, coming up from the washing. Each has its twin; not one of them is alone. Your lips are like a scarlet ribbon; your mouth is lovely. Your temples behind your veil are like the halves of a pomegranate. Your neck is like the tower of David, built with courses of stone; on it hang a thousand shields, all of them shields of warriors. Your breasts are like two fawns, like twin fawns of a gazelle that browse among the lilies. Until the day breaks and the shadows flee, I will go to the mountain of myrrh and to the hill of incense. You are altogether beautiful, my darling; there is no flaw in you.

You cannot read the Song of Solomon without blushing, for it is the account of an intimate conversation between a man and his wife. This passage indicates that communication has always been the key to a successful marriage, as we have reiterated throughout this book. The modern couple will do well to heed our words, as well as those of the wisdom writer from 3,100 years ago!

8. **Song of Solomon 5:10-16:** My beloved is radiant and ruddy, outstanding among ten thousand. His head is purest gold; his hair is wavy and black as a raven. His eyes are like doves by the water streams, washed in milk, mounted like jewels. His cheeks are like beds of spice yielding perfume. His lips are like lilies dripping with myrrh. His arms are rods of gold set with topaz. His body is like polished ivory decorated with lapis lazuli. His legs are pillars of marble set on bases of pure gold. His appearance is like Lebanon, choice as its cedars. His mouth is sweetness itself; he is altogether lovely. This is my beloved, this is my friend, daughters of Jerusalem.

This passage continues the steamy dialogue between the woman and her man. This tells us that women are to pay attention to a man's ego and to inform him regularly that he is the only one for her—and then back it up with concrete reasons!

9. **Song of Solomon 7:1-10:** How beautiful your sandaled feet, O prince's daughter! Your graceful legs are like jewels, the work of an artist's hands. Your navel is a rounded goblet that never lacks blended wine.

Your waist is a mound of wheat encircled by lilies. Your breasts are like two fawns, like twin fawns of a gazelle. Your neck is like an ivory tower. Your eyes are the pools of Heshbon by the gate of Bath Rabbim. Your nose is like the tower of Lebanon looking toward Damascus. Your head crowns you like Mount Carmel. Your hair is like royal tapestry; the king is held captive by its tresses. How beautiful you are and how pleasing, my love, with your delights. Your stature is like that of the palm, and your breasts like clusters of fruit. I said, "I will climb the palm tree; I will take hold of its fruit." May your breasts be like clusters of grapes on the vine, the fragrance of your breath like apples, and your mouth like the best wine. May the wine go straight to my beloved, flowing gently over lips and teeth. I belong to my beloved, and his desire is for me.

By now, you should have the idea that the Bible is not ashamed to record intimate talk between a husband and wife. If God is not embarrassed, then we should not be either! Both the husband and wife must seek ways to build up their spouse with words that are meaningful to the spouse.

10. **1 Peter 2:17**: Show proper respect to everyone, love the family of believers, fear God, honor the emperor.

We admit that this verse is not about marriage, but it mentions an important aspect of every successful marriage, and that is respect. Husbands and wives must manifest respect for one another, especially in front of their children and other family members.

11. **1 Peter 3:7**: Husbands, in the same way be considerate as you live with your wives, and treat them with respect as the weaker partner and as heirs with you of the gracious gift of life, so that nothing will hinder your prayers.

Yes, the wife is weaker physically in most cases, but that does not mean she is inferior to her husband. Peter urged husbands to be considerate and respectful of their wives. If the husbands refuse, then God will not hear their prayers. Imagine that: God will refuse to listen to any husband who does not honor his wife. That indicates how important it is for husbands to treat their wives as equals and partners, not slaves or mistresses.

Those are some of the biblical passages that we refer to from time to time in our teaching and counseling, particularly where intimacy and sex are discussed. We encourage you to do your own study and find references that are important to you and your marriage, not just about your physical but also concerning your spiritual condition as life partners. . If you don't know where to search, go online, ask a pastor, or attend a biblical marriage seminar. Better yet, use this book to lead your own small group devoted to the study of marriage. Even though you are a modern couple, you will find an endless source of timeless wisdom from the biblical writers.

Now that we have covered sex and intimacy, it's time to move on to the topic of finances, an issue that causes more stress among modern couples than any other.

CHAPTER 14

PARENTING AND CHILDREN

When dealing with parenting and children, it's the biblical position that parents are to bring up their children in what's referred to as "the discipline and instruction of the Lord." As believers in Christ, we must view our children as a blessing and not a liability. We also can't see them as those who are supposed to serve us, their parents, but instead are to be served by the parents who are even to lay up an inheritance for the children, as the Bible says: "A good person leaves an inheritance for their children's children, but a sinner's wealth is stored up for the righteous" (Proverbs 13:22).

As parents, we can easily become self-absorbed in our own personal desires and forget that God has called us to raise our children in a godly fashion to know and serve Him. Our children did not ask to be born or brought into this world. If we have them, then we should make them a priority. When we get caught up in our own personal happiness, too often our children suffer. Proverbs 22:6 tells us that we should influence and shape our children, and it has a fantastic promise attached to it when we do: "Start children off on the way they should go, and even when they are old they will not turn from it." If we are diligent to raise our children properly, in most cases they will remember and walk out what we taught them when they are older.

It is interesting to us that some parents don't begin to think about church involvement until their children get old enough to be taught. Then the parents pay attention to their need to raise children with ethics and values. We should do our best to raise our children in the church and in a Christian environment. That being said, there are questions we need to ask ourselves about how and what are the considerations for raising our children, and that entails more than just clothing and feeding. We have to make decisions about where our children will go to school. Do we enroll them in a Christian or private school? Do we home-school them? Our personal philosophy is that we're not opposed to bringing up kids in the public schools. One of the reasons why it may be beneficial to bring kids up in a public school is that it often exposes them to the diversity of thought and personality that a lot of the private and Christian schools don't have.

The Bible also talks to us about the rod, which is a big point of debate as to whether or not to spank children. If you follow what the Bible says, spanking the child is not the wrong thing to do. We believe in spanking, but with strict limitations. We don't believe spanking should be used as punishment, but should be used as discipline—and it's important to understand the difference between those two.

The problem with spanking is when it's done in anger, it becomes a beating, which is punishment. What the goal of spanking is to teach the child that there are implications and ramifications for his or her disobedience in life. For example, if a child has been told not to run out into traffic, that isn't simply the parent's preference. It is for the child's good. Thus, if the child is spanked when they run out into the street after they have been taught not to do so, it is so they will hopefully remember the next time they have an inclination to run.

Ultimately, a parent is teaching a child to obey the Lord, imparting the truth to the child that there are serious and possible eternal consequences for disobedience. The spanking helps the child hear the parent's voice so that they will carry that attentiveness over to what the Lord is directing them to do in His word.

Here are a few verses that support what we are saying:

- "A rod and a reprimand impart wisdom, but a child left undisciplined disgraces its mother" (Proverbs 29:15).

- "Folly is bound up in the heart of a child, but the rod of discipline will drive it far away" (Proverbs 22:15).

- "Do not withhold discipline from a child; if you punish them with the rod, they will not die" (Proverbs 23:13).

- "Blows and wounds scrub away evil, and beatings purge the inmost being" (Proverbs 20:30).

Children need to know and learn the difference between punishment and discipline. Children must be taught that when parents discipline them, they are doing it because they love them, and also that's what the Bible directed us as parents to do. We're disciplined by God because He loves us. Therefore, we should teach the child that we are doing what we do because we love them. That brings a responsibility to the parent to discipline in love, not to punish in anger. The old saying associated with parents who discipline their children saying, "This hurts me more than it hurts you." Until that's true, the parent should be very careful when they administer corporal discipline. In fact, if they can't say that, then they should not physically discipline at all.

There are other means of discipline. Spanking isn't the only thing a parent can do as far as discipline goes. Other disciplines include taking away privileges, additional duties around the home, limitation of freedoms, and apologizing and making restitution for wrongs committed. When you discipline a child, you want to let them know that the behavior is not acceptable and that you want and need to see a change.

During our upbringing, spanking was a prominent way of discipline. The rod was not spared. When we were told it was going to hurt our parents more than us, we didn't understand that. Children must be taught to know that they're Christian children being raised in a Christian home, and there is a certain behavior expected of them that is not expected of their non-Christian friends. That's so when our children say, "Everyone is doing this or that," they are taught not to give in to peer pressure but to consider what God would have them do at any given moment.

Discipline is a negative word for most people, but the biblical perspective is positive. We know we are disciplined because God loves us, as it tells us in Hebrews:

> And have you completely forgotten this word of encouragement that addresses you as a father addresses his son? It says, "My son, do not make light of the Lord's discipline, and do not lose heart when he rebukes you, because the Lord disciplines the one he loves, and he chastens everyone he accepts as his son." Endure hardship as discipline; God is treating you as his children. For what children are not disciplined by their father? If you are not disciplined—and everyone undergoes discipline—then you are not legitimate, not true sons and daughters at all.
>
> Moreover, we have all had human fathers who disciplined us and we respected them for it. How much more should we submit to the Father of spirits and live! They disciplined us for a little while as they thought best; but God disciplines us for our good, in order that we may share in his holiness. No discipline seems pleasant at the time, but painful. Later on, however, it produces a harvest of righteousness and peace for those who have been trained by it (Hebrews 12:5-11).

Please understand, however, that we are not talking about abusing or taking out anger on a child. We're talking about doing it from the point of view of love and not punishment. That carries a lot of responsibility, because God has called us to be His authority figures in our home. God has called the parent to be His representative to the children. Therefore, the parent must do things in a godly manner as God would have them done.

We also encourage parents not to underestimate the spirituality of their children, which is another important reason why the children must be exposed to religious instruction. There are many biblical example of children to whom the Lord spoke and revealed His purpose for them. Parents should be attentive from the child's earliest age to recognize and help develop each child's gifts and life purpose.

As an example of this, we use the story of Moses, whose parents had to face the edict of the Egyptian king who said all male children had to be killed. Moses' parents did not want to comply with this decree for reasons explained in the New Testament: "By faith Moses' parents hid him for three months after he was born, because they saw he was no ordinary child, and they were not afraid of the king's edict" (Hebrews 11:23). Moses' parents saw something in their child and it caused them to take steps to ensure that his purpose would be fulfilled.

It is easy to get distracted from our child's God-given purpose when we as parents have to deal with their mess as they grow up. We can lose track of the promise that if we do our job, they will walk in the way we teach them *eventually*. Moses' parents saw that he was special, not because he was a cute baby, but because God had a purpose for him. Therefore, they took special precautions to make sure their baby boy would have a chance to fulfill his purpose.

We encourage parents to take the long view where their children are concerned and do all they can to direct them on the life path God has assigned for them. That requires that the parents not dissipate all the family's resources, or create dysfunction to the point where the children are always at the mercy of the parents' neediness or problems. We are not advocating that couples should serve their children at the exclusion of their own needs, but to recognize that the children have legitimate needs, just like Mom and Dad, and for them to make room for their children in the life and attention.

There are two significant passages concerning children that we point out and emphasize in the New Testament. They are:

1. **Ephesians 6:1-4.** Children, obey your parents in the Lord, for this is right. "Honor your father and mother"—which is the first commandment with a promise—"so that it may go well with you and that you may enjoy long life on the earth." Fathers, do not exasperate your children; instead, bring them up in the training and instruction of the Lord.

2. **Colossians 3:20-21.** Children, obey your parents in everything, for this pleases the Lord. Fathers, do not embitter your children, or they will become discouraged

The first passage stresses that it is in the children's best interests to honor their parents, for God is watching and promises to bless the children when they do so. It doesn't mean their parents are perfect or that children should look past bad or inappropriate behavior as they seek to honor their parents. It does mean that God chose that man and woman to be parents, and they should honor them accordingly. That passage also gives a warning to fathers not to wear the children out with too much discipline or too many rules. It does admonish fathers to oversee their children's training in the things of the Lord.

The second passage reiterates what was written in the first one, and it is interesting that Paul wrote this to non-Jewish parents and children. In other words, obedience to parents was not simply a Jewish directive, it pertained to all children everywhere. That would include the children of modern couples.

We truthfully don't spend a lot of time on this subject because many of the people who attend our seminars either don't have children, or their children are older, sometimes even married with their own children. We try to lay the foundation to make couples aware that children will add a whole new dimension to their relationship, and that they will need help and input in that area of life as well as the others we have discussed. The problem with children is they don't come with an owner's manual! We also recommend many good books and other resources for parents so they can access the help they need. We will close this discussion with two subjects that have increasingly emerged in our seminars—blended families and the empty nest. Let's proceed to those topics but first, let's review:

1. Parents are expected to discipline their children.

2. There is a difference between discipline and punishment.

3. Ultimately, parents are to train their children to obey the Lord. Learning to obey their parents is the means to that end.

CHAPTER 15

BLENDED FAMILIES AND THE EMPTY NEST

We like to think that everyone in a family is going to get along like we witnessed on older TV shows where it seemed like they were always one, big happy family. In real life, that is seldom the case, especially when the families are blended. A blended family is one where there are children from a previous marriage or relationship who are living with a mother or father figure who is not his or her true birth parent. A lot of the responsibility falls on the stepparent to make adjustments in a blended family. Some of the things that need to happen in a blended family have already been discussed. Communication, roles, finances and discipline will have to be addressed. One of the more important practices is communication. In the blended family, the stepparent needs to find time to talk with and participate in activities together with their stepchildren. Since they don't have a relationship that has unfolded from birth, they need to exert the effort to develop one.

Speaking from our personal experience, the transition isn't always as smooth as couples would like it to be. It can be traumatic for the stepchild and the natural child when they come together. The natural child was the one who was getting the attention, but all of a sudden there may be a sibling with whom he or she has to share time and resources—and maybe even a sleeping room. Parents need to focus on the relationship with their stepchild and do whatever it takes to build as strong of a bond as possible, without neglecting their biological children.

The stepparent must also give the stepchildren an opportunity to speak their mind and tell both parents how they feel about a situation, even if it is painful and the stepparent must bite his or her tongue clear through while listening. This blended family is a new team, and that means time has to be invested in building the team and developing the relationships. When we got married, we worked hard to have fun and laugh together with all our children as a blended family. We didn't want to steamroll one or the other child. What we wanted to do was build relationships.

In the last chapter, we discussed discipline, and sometimes in blended families stepparents may hold back on discipline because they don't want anyone to think they are being harder on the stepchildren. Then they will have to hear, "You're not really my mother or father." The stepparent must consistently show that they're always supporting the family as a unit. We did that from the start of our relationship. We never really thought "stepchildren." Helen called my [Jack's] sons "my sons." We recently attended the twentieth wedding anniversary of "our" oldest son and it was a marvelous occasion. The entire blended family all sat together. That's the result of doing what we talked about—building relationships—over the years.

When Jack's middle son came to live with us, he went right into the room with his stepbrother, and that's the way we presented it. I [Jack] informed him that there were consequences for bad behavior and we were going to address it. I [Jack] would not reward bad behavior if he did something wrong, but that applied across the board for everyone. But also, we offered positive reinforcement when that was warranted as well. Our main strategy for the blended family was to treat everyone like family.

Like it or not, the ex-spouse or parent of your children is part of the family, even though they are not present. We never talked about or disrespected our former spouses. We honored their role in our children's lives. Helen calls Jack's children's mother her "wife-in-law." Everyone picked up on that.

Children want and need to see their parents getting along, and that means *all* their parents. Obviously there are going to be conflicts in the relationships, but the children still want to see them get along. We have to be careful to remind each other that if we love the children, we'll make every effort to be respectful to one another.

One of the most important things in parenting, and especially stepparenting, is that the parent has to admit when he or she was wrong when a mistake was made. The spouse needs to have the attitude of "let's move on" when his or her partner errs with the child that is not his or her own. There is one standard of behavior for *all* the children and if that's not in play, then the offending parent needs to own up to his or her mistake and acknowledge that there has to be one standard for *all* the children.

This means that the parents have to be united and be applying all the previous rungs of the marriage ladder that we have described in this book. They have to communicate, define roles (even for the children), make decisions, and settle conflicts. That means the parents have to pray and seek the Lord, and the children have to share in the responsibility of creating a harmonious household.

We didn't ever think it was a good idea to bring up too many of the painful issues from the past with our former spouses, or even discuss the happy times, for that matter. Some happy discussion is okay, because you have a common bond in the family from the past that you cannot escape or ignore. For instance, there were pictures that were shared during our son's 20th anniversary on a slide show that pictured him when he was young. That included times when I [Jack] was with his mother. We were able to smile, however, because we saw the good times, but we were always careful not to bring up too many past issues that caused us to separate and break up as a couple. We did, however, accentuate and highlight the good times we have shared with the children.

We approached blending from a Christian perspective. We prayed as a family, and everyone went to church together. God commands and instructs us how to behave as Christians, and we adopted that behavior. What does the Bible tell us to do? Our first goal was to love. Our children needed to see us live out a life of love as Christians, and that's what we tried to do. We have been successful, although we have made mistakes. God has been gracious to us, and now we're in a place where everyone is comfortable.

When we facilitate for couples who have not yet been as successful at blending, we go and rely on the Bible to teach people how to treat and respect one another. The Bible tells us repeatedly to live, forgive, forebear with, and be gentle with all. We're commanded to love our neighbors as ourselves. That's what we stand on, not just with people who are not in our family, but especially with those who are. It's doable and we've seen it done, but it is a sacrifice for us all. We did it in order to raise healthy young adults.

One of the verses to back up what we're saying is found in Titus 2:7 (ESV): "To show yourself in all respect to be a model of good works and in your teaching show integrity and dignity." In all of the things we did and do, the Bible tell us we need to show integrity and dignity in how we deal with one another.

We are not naïve. We know that some children were deeply wounded in their early years or during their parents' separation. That caused them to be angry, and that anger is not going to go away after the blended family goes to see a counselor or goes out to dinner together. It is going to take time, prayer, counseling, patience, and sometimes what seems like a process best described as two steps forward and three steps back. If you are facing a difficult, seemingly impossible situation with your children, natural or step, take it one day at a time, pray, and trust the Lord that in time, it will all work out for the good. Until then, life can be unbearable and only your faith will get you through the day.

Empty Nest

The empty nest is a season in a couple's relationship when the children are grown and out of the house. This can cause some issues for both partners, but if the family is blended, it can have a deep impact on the biological parent. There are surveys conducted to show there are more divorces that come after the nest is empty, because the parents have to face and deal with each other after their focus has been on their children for so long. Once the children are gone, the parents have to fall in love all over again. We told our son at his 20th anniversary celebration that he needed to fall in love often; it just has to be with the same person!

The truth of the matter is, the husband and wife are different people than when they first met, started dating, or from when they first got married. People grow and evolve, so you have to embrace the changes, and a lot of times that can be traumatic. One man told us that he used to buy gifts for his wife, but her tastes changed over the years. After a few wrong purchases, he gave up and stopped gift giving. The problem was that his wife saw this as rejection, so there was tension between them.

What should they have done? The husband should have spent the time to discover his wife's new tastes and desires for gifts. The wife should have asked why he stopped giving, and would have learned it had nothing to do with love. He was feeling failure and she was sensing rejection. If they had taken the time to communicate, they would have realized they were changing and needed to devote the time and energy to keep up with who their partner was today, not who they had been yesterday.

When the children are gone, it is a good time for couples to find new interests they can do together, things like dance lessons, travel, classes, or a special craft. Above all else, the couple must work to communicate with one another and create an environment of peace and harmony in the home. One of the partners may need some counseling to help with the transition and if that's the case, the other should be supportive and patient. The parents must also not continue to be so involved in their children's lives that they [the children] can't have lives of their own. When it's time for them to move on, both parents must permit them to do so, and refocus their energies on their marriage.

Studies show that people who are married actually live longer. Now you may read that and believe it's because they are happy and in love. That may be the case, but it's also because they can keep one another accountable where health is concerned. They can remind one another of tests and checkups that are due. They can be supportive when one or the other happens to be ill. Finally, they can challenge one another to keep the weight off and the exercise regular! Yes, the empty nest is a time when couples face things they have never had to face before, but if they do it together, it can be another meaningful chapter in the book of their relationship.

Here are some things to remember where blended families and the empty nest are concerned:

1. In blended families, parents must work to have a consistent standard for all children.

2. Communication is especially important in blended families.

3. Parents should be preparing for the day when their children are gone and it is back to just the couple being in the home.

Before we close this book, our work would not be complete if we neglected a discussion of another potential problem in a relationship and that is the issue of money. Let's spend a chapter talking about that critical topic.

CHAPTER 16

FINANCE AND BUDGETING

Many studies show that the main issue that causes stress and divorce is the issue of money. A lot of the tension that comes up in a marriage or relationship are money-based, both because of the presence or a lack of finances. Therefore, we spend some time talking to the modern couple about their spending habits and ways in which they can become more responsible. In our seminar session about money, we try to help them recognize their need for both a savings and spending plan. Our goal is to introduce some tools to help with planning and emphasize the importance of trying to follow a plan.

Before we get to the plan, however, there are other issues that the couple must discuss and decide—again involving the communication skills we imparted to them earlier. Will they have a joint bank account or keep things separate? Who will pay what and when? When happens when the money runs out before the month ends; who covers the deficit? Will they have separate or group investments?

We found that living with debt can be difficult and bring great stress on any couple, especially if their income lessens while the debt does not. School loans have become a huge problem for couples who at times have a combined debt total in excess of $100,000. That's going to require the equivalent of a monthly house payment for many years to come to see that debt retired. There are times when couples need to resort to a debt consolidation program, which requires great discipline and commitment. If you miss one payment in those programs, the organization can terminate the service, so this is nothing to play with or treat lightly.

Whether or not the couple uses a debt reduction service, they must learn some basic principles where debt is concerned. They should not only make the minimum payment due on any debt if they want to pay it off as quickly as possible. Sometimes one or the other partner can look for temporary sources of income, such as a second job, military reserve duty, or liquidation of assets like coin collections or other things of value.

We found that having a plan in place is the best thing. If a couple has a plan, at least they have *something* to refer to and adjust as their financial situation changes. We also point out (and want them both to realize) that rarely are both parties identically the same as far as spending habits are concerned. One may be a natural saver while the other is a natural spender. Having a plan helps alleviate some of the issues that arise from that tension. We have people list their expenses, itemize things, and find out where they are, or where they are not. We work to make sure the couple sets some financial goals, for we want them to be goal-oriented where finances are concerned so they can stay disciplined and in one accord.

It's important to have goals. Goals provide meaning and purpose in life, so they should identify objectives and set goals for a couple without eliminating personal goals. We know that sometimes one partner falls prey to impulse shopping, and that habit needs to be isolated and adjusted. If you are a spender, that may be a habit you need to break. Most debt didn't happen overnight and it won't go away overnight. If couples stick to the plan or return to the plan if they have deviated, however, they will eventually be victorious.

Some husbands turn the money management over to their wives once they get paid, because the wife is a better manager. That goes back to our teaching on roles and responsibilities, for it's important to know who is better at managing money, and who is better at managing risk. The partner who excels in the latter role should be the one who leads the way on investments. These roles are not gender specific, but are rather gift or strength specific. The couple should discover who enjoys doing what, and who is good at doing those things. Sometimes the roles will reverse after the couple has been together for a longer period of time. In some cases, depending where they are in life, one may not be able to physically or mentally able to handle the responsibilities that he or she once had.

To provide a simple overview of what we recommend in our seminars, we suggest couples follow a 10/10/80 plan: pay 10% as a tithe to their church or charity; save 10%; and devote 80% to their living expenses—and learn to live within that 80% with no debt. We find many people find it a challenge to save money. At times, the couple must look for ways to increase their income, but in the meantime, they need to watch expenses and plan for emergencies. One of the things we discovered is that the Bible warns us about life storms. If you can prepare for the inevitable storm, you have a better chance of weathering that storm. In a lot of cases, the couples aren't prepared and it brings on additional difficulties.

As we did in the chapter on sex and intimacy, we want to include some of the passages we refer to when we teach and facilitate our session on finances. We will present them to you and urge you to look at them to study for yourself. We just want to give you a brief synopsis of what we see in these verses that have helped us and can therefore help others.

1. **1 Timothy 6:6-10.** But godliness with contentment is great gain. For we brought nothing into the world, and we can take nothing out of it. But if we have food and clothing, we will be content with that. Those who want to get rich fall into temptation and a trap and into many foolish and harmful desires that plunge people into ruin and destruction. For the love of money is a root of all kinds of evil. Some people, eager for money, have wandered from the faith and pierced themselves with many griefs.

The modern couple is often under intense pressure to spend on vacations, homes, cars, technology, weddings, gifts and just about anything else that money can buy. TV screens that were once cutting-edge are now obsolete and a new one is available with no payments due for six months! The passage above speaks to the matter of contentment—being satisfied with what you have. That includes being satisfied with your income, guarding against the desire to get rich. That desire can lead to workaholic lifestyles, risky investments, and just plan envy of those who are richer than you—and there is always someone who has amassed more.

Notice in that passage that money is not the problem; it is the love of money that is the problem. That love of money has caused many to stray away from faith and church, and when that happens, the stress on the modern couple only increases as they lose a lifeline for help and encouragement.

2. **1 Timothy 6:17-19:** Command those who are rich in this present world not to be arrogant nor to put their hope in wealth, which is so uncertain, but to put their hope in God, who richly provides us with everything for our enjoyment. Command them to do good, to be rich in good deeds, and to be generous and willing to share. In this way they will lay up treasure for themselves as a firm foundation for the coming age, so that they may take hold of the life that is truly life.

We have encountered some modern couples who do have significant incomes and possessions. They have been able to afford nice things and live in beautiful homes and drive expensive cars. There is nothing wrong with that, but we do remind them that those things are fleeting. Houses fall into sinkholes, cars wear out and age, and the stock market rises and falls. Families are not to direct all their income and wealth into personal consumption, but are to use their fleeting wealth to invest in good deeds that will pay dividends for all eternity.

3. **Matthew 6:24:** "No one can serve two masters. Either you will hate the one and love the other, or you will be devoted to the one and despise the other. You cannot serve both God and money."

There is no way around this truth: No one can have money as a master and serve anyone or anything else. In this context, Jesus said that no one can serve money and then claim to serve God. Those two are mutually exclusive. Money is a means to an end, and not an end unto itself!

4. **James 5:13:** Your gold and silver are corroded. Their corrosion will testify against you and eat your flesh like fire. You have hoarded wealth in the last days.

A rich man died and two of his friends stood looking at his body in the casket. One asked, "How much did he leave?" and the other answered, "All of it!" You cannot take any money with you, so it is best to have some to leave for posterity and use the rest to build up riches in heaven.

5. **Luke 12:15:** Then he [Jesus] said to them, "Watch out! Be on your guard against all kinds of greed; life does not consist in an abundance of possessions."

How much is too much? You can only wear one pair of shoes and one belt at a time. Is there a need for fifty pair of shoes and twenty belts? Probably not, but it is a subtle trap to accumulate more and more, hoarding and protecting it. There was a bumper sticker years ago that stated, "He who dies with the most toys wins!" There was another that countered, "He who dies with the most toys—still dies!"

6. **Colossians 3:5:** Put to death, therefore, whatever belongs to your earthly nature: sexual immorality, impurity, lust, evil desires and greed, which is idolatry.

It is interesting that Paul equated greed with idolatry. It is a humorous picture of someone bowing down before a dollar bill, but that is the exact picture of greed—wanting more and more. That desire for more and more should be for God and His ways, not for money, possessions, and wealth.

7. **Proverbs 3:9-10:** Honor the LORD WITH YOUR WEALTH, with the firstfruits of all your crops; then your barns will be filled to overflowing, and your vats will brim over with new wine.

The wisdom writer in Proverbs instructed people to honor God with wealth. How can anyone honor God with money? They can do so by being generous rather than being stingy.

8. **Proverbs 10:4:** Lazy hands make for poverty, but diligent hands bring wealth.

We know too many people who gamble or are looking for a quick way to gain wealth. Some even do that in church when they give to an appeal that says, "Give $1,000 and God will give you much more!" There is no meaningful way to gain wealth than to do honorable work to earn it and then to save and invest wisely, including investments in God and His people.

9. **Proverbs 10:22:** The blessing of the Lord brings wealth, without painful toil for it.

We have counseled many couples who seldom see one another or their children due to work schedules. While men are more susceptible, we see more and more women falling prey to this tendency to working long hours to try and get ahead. This verse states that God will prosper people and He won't make them sell their soul to a company to obtain their prosperity.

10. **Proverbs 11:25:** A generous person will prosper; whoever refreshes others will be refreshed.

Generosity is a wonderful trait for couples to develop. This can be exercised through giving or through hospitality, which is sharing what you have in your home with others. The promise in this verse is that those who are generous will be refreshed themselves.

11. **Proverbs 22:9:** The generous will themselves be blessed, for they share their food with the poor.

Most people think of themselves as "poor," and quote the old adage that "charity begins at home." This verse states the opposite is true. Charity is finding people who are in worse financial condition than you and helping them. When you do that, you will be blessed.

12. **Proverbs 11:28:** Those who trust in their riches will fall, but the righteous will thrive like a green leaf.

It is easy to put your trust in your bank account, or your investments, or your ability to earn money. This verse warns you not to put your trust in riches or wealth, for they are here today and gone tomorrow. Special note: You may not think of yourself as "wealthy" so then these warnings cannot be for you. If you live in the U.S., however, you are numbered among the wealthy of the world. Just ask someone in Africa who eats one meal a day, and who earns $150 per month. You may be spending all you have, and thus you have little left at the end of the month—but that doesn't make you poor.

13. **Proverbs 23:5:** Cast but a glance at riches, and they are gone, for they will surely sprout wings and fly off to the sky like an eagle.

Once again, the wisdom writer warned his reader that money is like a bird that can one day sprout wings and fly away. Don't put your trust in something so fickle and temporary.

14. **Proverbs 27:24:** For riches do not endure forever, and a crown is not secure for all generations.

Riches do not last forever!

15. **Proverbs 19:17:** Whoever is kind to the poor lends to the Lord, and

he will reward them for what they have done.

This verse adds an interesting twist to the benefit of giving to the poor: When you do, you are actually lending to the Lord and he will reward you! That should make you want to find some poor people in the world and help them, especially those who can in no way repay or reward you. When that occurs, God will reward you.

16. **Proverbs 21:17:** Whoever loves pleasure will become poor; whoever loves wine and olive oil will never be rich.

Our culture today attaches a high value on leisure and workaholic lifestyles crave some down time. This verse warns not to become addicted to pleasure, however that is defined according to your tastes.

Perhaps you did not know the Bible had so much to say about money and wealth. In fact, there is plenty more where that came from. We simply wanted to share with you some of the points we make in our seminar so you can do some study on your own. Once you begin, there are plenty of other resources that can guide you through a more thorough study of finances. We don't only recommend, however, that you study the Bible. We encourage you to secure the services of a good financial planner, even if it is just for your monthly budget and certainly for certain long-term investments. The large percentage of couples reach retirement age today and have little else to rely on for income than social security. That's not healthy for their relationship and for their quality of life in the latter years.

Now that you have read this chapter, we encourage you to go back and read the first part again, now that you have had a healthy dose of biblical wisdom on finances. Ask yourselves the questions: Are we saving? Are we generous? Are we using our income to honor God and store up treasures in heaven? Are we helping the poor? Do we spend all we make on ourselves and our own needs and wants? Are we consumed by debt? As you reflect and answer those questions honestly, it can help you make some changes, first in your thinking and approach toward wealth, then in your spending habits, and ultimately in your lifestyle. If you do that, you will be courageously facing one of the main causes of marital stress, and that is money.

Let's review some of the more significant things to remember in this chapter:

1. The partner who handles the money should be the one who is gifted and skilled to do so.

2. Decisions must be made as to how each couple will handle their finances concerning joint accounts, investments, and budgeting.

3. The Bible has a lot to say about money and a wise couple will heed its counsel!

There you have it—that is what we do when we have couples for eight weeks! We have seen it happen over and over again, however, that once the eight weeks are up, the journey has just begun and the couples tend to stay connected to us. That is a joy for us, for we know that once we have taught and facilitated, there is still much work to do to make a happy marriage. The modern couple faces unprecedented challenges from a culture that is saturated with technology, addicted to busy-ness, stressed by materialism, and tormented by an attitude that says, "If I don't get what I want, I'll sue!" And that desire to sue can be for a divorce with few questions asked.

CONCLUSION

We encourage couples to read everything they can concerning marriage, parenting, the various stages of child development, with a view toward how it is going to impact their relationship. We can't discuss and provide answers on all the topics in this book—even when people are attend every session. We don't encourage couples to adopt everything they read, but encourage discussing it once they have both read the same thing.

We further encourage couples to attend church and to take advantage of marriage or parenting programs offered by their church or other churches. There are also some wonderful instructional DVDs on the market. The point is that marriage is a lifelong challenge and requires lifelong effort to maximize the relationship.

It's been said that divorce in the church is the same rate as outside the church, which is 50% of first-time marrieds (higher for those with multiple marriages). That's a myth that's been going around for a long time. Several studies have found that divorce in the church is in the 30-40% range. That's still way too high, but it points to how important church attendance and involvement is. It is vital to find the right church because it helps shape you as you live out your values where marriage is concerned.

When God is at the center of a marriage, it will work, but He has to be at the core. Couples are going to disagree and have arguments. All of the things we have discussed in marriage are going to happen—and them some things will happen that we did not discuss. We make every effort to live by the word of God. If you pray, God will strengthen that relationship with Him and in turn, with one another.

For couples who are dating, we encourage them to pray as well. Marriage is tough enough with the right partner; no one needs to be in a relationship with the wrong person. Those couples need to know that this man, this woman is the one for me, the one with whom I will spend the rest of my life. Some people dated and married wrong because they just didn't know any better. You can know better, especially if you are in church.

Our thanks to our family, to the Center for Urban Biblical Ministry and Mrs. Karla Byrd, to Mrs. Val Ford (who was our mentor for The Marriage Works), to Dr. John Stanko, who is our friend and editor, and to all those who have allowed us to "experiment" on them as we learned to teach and facilitate. We have learned a lot in the process, and we know we could not have done what we did without many hands helping us. Finally, we thank God and our Lord Jesus Christ, who spared us from the misery of a life separated from God so that we may serve Him and His people. We want to spend the rest of our days equipping modern couples for success, and it is to that end that we dedicate this book. Thank you, and thank You, Lord!

www.ingramcontent.com/pod-product-compliance
Lightning Source LLC
Chambersburg PA
CBHW082358270326
41935CB00013B/1667